Born to Be A Sports Agent

Born to Be A Sports Agent

Jill McBride Baxter

ISBN-978-1-7333444-3-2(pbk)
ISBN-978-1-7333444-4-9 (hbk)
ISBN-978-1-7333444-5-6 (ebook)
LCCN: 2019918903

1st edition, November 2019

Cover Design by Michael Scott, MAS Graphic Arts

Photograph on Cover by Meredith Elaine Photography

Jill McBride Baxter books may be purchased in bulk by email jillbaxter@me.com or 559-250-0151
www.jillmcbridebaxter.com.

Published by Jill McBride Baxter, Sports Law Attorney
An imprint of Jill McBride Baxter

Dedication

To my clients: You are the reason I get up every day and I love every minute representing you.

To Grace DeWitt, Douglas Digital, you are the best addition to my team and I appreciate your dedication and feedback!

To my sister Kelly who was there for me and our girls every step of the way!

To my parents: I got lucky to get these two as parents. I wish everyone had them as parents—the world would be a better place! Particularly my mom!

To all the badass women and friends I have met along the way!

To my girls, Kelly and McKenzie, I am so proud of you every day for the bright independent women you have become.

To my husband! You are a great father, mentor, coach, and partner in life. Thanks for loving my adventurous spirit and passion for work! Lastly your cooking and laundry skills the best! xoxo Jill

Table of Contents

Introduction

I grew up on a football field. Now, you might be thinking, *Really? You mean you literally grew up on a football field, like right there on the 50-yard line*? Well, maybe not literally, but it sure feels like it! And for those of you who are coach's kids like me, we've been going to practices since the day we were born so you know what I'm talking about.

This book is a culmination of my three decades (wow, that sounds like a long time) of being a sports agent. It's not that I woke up one day and decided to become a sports agent. My entire life has been encased in football, and I'm happy it turned out that way. I feel like I've actually lived three lives; one as a coach's kid, one as a coach's wife, and one as a sports agent, but, really, all three have been and continue to be a massive part of who I am as a human being.

What you can expect from the pages of this book is an inside peek, no, more than a peek; a magnifying glass image of what my life has been like, how it has developed, and how I've stayed relevant through three decades as one of the only female sports agents in the industry. You don't just wake up one day and shout, "Hey world, I want to be a female in a male-dominated business!" You evolve as a person, and you end up asking, "What was I put on this earth to do? What is my place in this vast universe? What do I stand for? How can I help humanity solve their problems?" Then…it comes to you…simply by virtue of living a fulfilled life.

That's what happened to me. I was living life as a coach's kid; growing up on a university football field, running through the halls of various universities, and attending summer camps while Dad coached and Mom held down the fort, better than most I believe. I was entrenched in friendships and activities and deciding what my college major would be.

I decided to go to law school. As a law student, I was president of the Sports Law Forum and also played intramural sports. At the time, my dad had a player who needed a contract negotiated and he asked if I could help. Well, of course I could. Figuring things out had always been my strong suit so I took on the client and there I was…a sports agent…well, sort of. There's always more to the story and you will read about the "more" in this book.

In due time I became a wife and mother, blending my career with being there to support my husband and caring for my kids, taking them to their own activities and sports practices and games while my sports agent business continued to grow. Now, there was a ranch, complete with horses, a bunch of animals, a host of goings-on, a steady stream of clients and…me…transforming and transitioning through it all.

There's always an evolution of self in the lives we live. We are not the same person at 40 as we were at 25. Becoming stagnant is not part of the evolution, for that would be a fate worse than death. I believe my adventurous spirit and competitive nature has kept me vibrant and in the game. I have changed through the years; I've grown emotionally, mentally, and vocationally, I've made mistakes and celebrated victories, but through it all I've remained a courageous woman who goes out there and gets what she wants. My parents always made us feel like we could do anything. So we did.

I hope this book inspires you to do the same!

SEGMENT I

THE X'S AND O'S OF BEING SURROUNDED BY COACHES

Chapter 1

Growing Up a Coach's Kid

Now that I've been in the sports agent industry for almost three decades, I can honestly say that one of the most common questions I get is, "Why did you want to be a sports agent?" But to understand how I became a sports agent, and to realize why I've been able to navigate successfully as a female sports agent all these years, you need to get a picture of how I grew up…on a football field.

My parents met at San Jose State and got married when they were still in college. I was the middle child of the three of us kids. Of course, I could never forget my half-brother Danny. My dad and a young lady he knew during high school had Danny when they were teens, but we didn't grow up with him. In fact, Danny didn't even know about us until he was in high school himself, although we knew about him. He is in the baseball world. He is general manager for single A baseball, he's a high school AD, and he coaches football. He is very close to our family and so are his kids. Danny, unfortunately, didn't live with us or visit us until he was in college, and now his kids and grandkids live right by my parents.

My mom has shown me newspaper clippings of herself when she was pregnant with my brother Mike, literally standing on a football field, because my dad was a student coach by the time I was born. My parents lived in the married student housing at San Jose State University and that's really where it all began.

At that time, my parents, along with a bunch of other players who were also married, lived in what was called family dorms, which meant they all attended college, they helped babysit each other's kids; actually my mom helped babysit everybody's kids and my dad was either playing or student coaching. Today, most if not all of the old buildings have been torn down but there is history in those old buildings.

***

My mom always took us to practices and I remember that we kids were always running around my dad's office—to us it was a very normal way of life. After my dad finished his student coaching at San Jose State, he took his first football coaching job at Piedmont Hills High School. But it wasn't just football that he coached; he also coached baseball and taught remedial math. My parents moved to a neighborhood in San Jose and all their best friends, including the Adamses, bought houses on the same street. My mom, at that time, was a substitute teacher and my dad, well, he did a few different things to make a living. He delivered papers at four o'clock in the morning and then he would go to school and teach. That was my parents' life; it's what they had to do to make ends meet. Since all their friends lived on the same street, and the friends had kids too, we'd all go outside to play and didn't come back in until it was time for dinner, whether we were eating at home or at the Adamses' house. The Adamses had four kids and of course my parents had three so our families were super close, and we still are to this day; one of my best friends is Vikki Adams. The Adamses were not a coaching family; the father was an engineer, but still, our parents were good friends and when we moved different places, the Adamses, oddly enough, landed in the same region, which meant that we kids attended elementary school together and actually ended up going to high school together in Salt Lake City, Utah.

As coach's kids, we had a ton of freedom, unlike my own kids who lived a more structured lifestyle. We would all go outside and play different kinds of sports; we went swimming in the Adamses' pool, we rode bikes, and basically we just ran around until it was time to come home. I can honestly say we had a great childhood. And then football season would roll around once again and that meant every Saturday we were at a football game. This was normal for all of us.

After San Jose State, head coach Wayne Howard at Gavilan Junior College in Gilroy hired Dad as offensive coordinator and Dad made the daily 64-mile round-trip commute between San Jose and Gilroy. Dad was also the tennis coach although he had never played tennis. The funny thing is that under his leadership, the tennis team won a championship.

So for us kids summers involved my dad running camps at Gavilan; we'd go to work with Dad and then take swimming lessons and get involved in whatever other activities were going on at the camp. Since my dad also taught swimming in the summer, I learned how to swim really well. Again, all of this seemed very normal to us kids…it was our life and we enjoyed it.

My dad wasn't one of those parents who felt the need to closely supervise any of us so that meant we would run around the campus, going either to the gym, the workout room, talking to everybody, hanging out in his office, and talking to the other coaches. At the end of his working day, he'd pile us in the car and head back home. Life was pretty easy. When football season started back up we were constantly at practices or games because my mom drove us there to hang out with the other coaches' kids and she would visit with the other wives.

Various circumstances in my life from zero to eight years old would ultimately impact my eventual decision to enter the sports law field. The main thing was that my family and I were always on a football field. The second thing was that both my parents basically accepted everybody which actually made Dad a great recruiter. He is still a great recruiter! He did and still does identify with just about anybody which made for some interesting adventures. One particular story stands out.

I was with my dad one day when he got a call about one of his players. This player had decided to dig a hole in the backyard of the property that the players were living in while they were students at Gavilan. The player's idea was to dig a hole so they could cook a pig; something that is commonly done in Polynesian culture. However, in San Jose, California, it was obviously not a common practice when you're renting a house to dig a hole to make a pit to roast pigs.

The house they were renting belonged to our great friends, the Adamses, who lived across the street and were away for six months on a work project in Missouri. Apparently, the neighbors and the Adamses were not really happy about the hole and my dad was the person called on to sort out the problem. The players did fix the hole but I am pretty sure the entire neighborhood knew about the digging of the pit.

Another thing I remember is that since Dad was a recruiter, it was common for total strangers to stay at our house. One time somebody came to our house and was sleeping in the living room. I didn't know it at the time and I thought it was my dad so I jumped on the pull-out couch in our living room to give my dad a hug, and it was a strange man who, in turn, grabbed me, and basically scared the shit out of me. Eyes wide and heart thumping, I ran into my room as fast as I could and quickly slammed the door shut. I realized at that moment that not all strangers are nice—this guy was pretty scary. To this day I have no idea who he was.

But again, strangers living at our house was a common theme. If there was a recent graduate or anyone else who needed help and a place to live, my parents helped them. They formed bonds with people and because of that I have immense respect and admiration for my parents. They were and still are great parents! Even today, former players, coaches and GA's remain close to my parents.

We lived an interesting life because we were exposed to so many different people—our house was the house where everybody gathered.

During my time growing up, our life as a family was so fun and easy, at least to me it was, and I think my siblings would agree.

My competitive nature began displaying itself very early. My mom tells the story of when I was two years old in swimming lessons at Pioneer High School in San Jose. The instructor taught me how to swim in half an hour. My mom had stepped away from the pool for a moment or two and when she came back out I was standing on the high dive jumping off toward the instructor. My mom's audible gasp and wide eyes clearly showed she was petrified. The instructor told my mom, "Hey, Jill wanted to do it so I told her I would be right here to catch her."

Needless to say, I have always liked swimming and water, as does my dad. Again, my parents taught us not to be afraid of anything and I believe I've proved that over and over throughout my life.

My competitiveness had grown stronger by the time I was five years old. I would challenge the boys in my class to foot races, which I would always win, because frankly I was faster than the boys my age. That all changed when I ran track in high school. At that age, I couldn't beat them, at least not the track athletes. Looking back, though, in elementary school I was competitive on the playground in first, second and third grade and beyond; I was on the monkey bars during recess, and we also played four-square, hopscotch, and jacks—those were the popular activities when I was little and I was all in! When I got home from school I played catch with the boys with either the baseball or the football. If we weren't playing in some kind of ball game, we were swimming or riding our bikes or roller skating. In fact, every single year for Halloween I wore a cheerleader outfit and put on roller skates because I wanted to see how much candy I could get—I found early on that I could go a lot faster on the skates and get to a lot more houses in a shorter period of time; my competitive nature in full play.

I was always trying to figure out a better way to do things. I'll tell you, we were basically unsupervised most of the day, and one of the things we loved most was going over to Durene Adams' house. Durene didn't care if we raided her refrigerator to make peanut butter and jelly sandwiches—we would mess up her house all the time but she didn't seem to mind. If we weren't over at Durene's, we were over at the Bogenreifs' house, and even though Trish was a lot stricter as far as the messes we made, we always wanted to eat dinner over at Trish's house. Trish was a great cook!

The block we lived on from kindergarten to third grade was quite idyllic in many ways but the closeness and camaraderie we had with the other families and the lasting friendships we built were priceless. When I think about it now, as kids, we solved our own problems, our parents did not solve our problems for us, and I have to say that we sometimes came up with some pretty good… or bad…ideas, depending on how you looked at it.

My friend Bob was pretty good at creative problem solving. If his mother told him to clean up the room, he threw everything out the window, so there was a pile of random stuff outside his bedroom window. Bob also loved to take things apart and put them back together so if his parents bought some new gadget, Bob used to try to take the new gadget apart, and sometimes it wouldn't exactly go back together so well.

At the Adamses' house, Walt and Durene played the guitar and painted. Listening to their guitar playing inspired me to want to take guitar lessons. I was absolutely horrific at it, and that's when I discovered I had absolutely no musical talent whatsoever so the lessons were short-lived to say the least. The Adamses also had a pool which was a regular gathering place—and remember, this was California so the weather was much more conducive to year-round swimming.

Glad that guitar lessons were behind me, I focused my full attention on sports because they came much easier and felt immensely more natural. It was never hard for me to learn a sport; didn't matter which sport, I could usually do it. When windsurfing got big, we bought a windsurfer and learned how to windsurf. When Dad ended up as a tennis coach, we learned how to play tennis. Every single part of my life revolved around a sport and a season, but the season that was most significant was football. Even though my dad coached tennis, football, swimming, and baseball, his true love was actually baseball; there was always a baseball game on in our house.

***

The year I turned eight my family experienced our first major move away from our neighborhood because Wayne Howard had been hired as the head coach of the football program at UC Riverside. He promptly hired my dad as his assistant head coach.

The move felt pretty traumatic to all of us because we were close to everybody in the neighborhood on Allen Avenue. Now that Dad was coaching at UC Riverside he somehow convinced Mom to buy a cabin in the mountains, which was about a 30-minute drive down the mountain. My dad had grown up in Southgate, and as a kid, he always went up to Crestline in the summer, and if you're not familiar with Crestline, it's in the San Bernardino Mountains. The town encircles a beautiful lake. It's a coveted vacation destination complete with hiking trails and unparalleled Southern California sunsets. In spite of all that, my reality was that I was heading into fourth grade and being uprooted from a neighborhood block where there were lots of kids, and somebody to play with at all times.

After much protest and a few tears we moved to a cabin in Crestline and it became evident very quickly that pretty much everybody who had a cabin up there used it as their second home. That meant we were fairly isolated for the most part but the good thing was because of the isolation I grew to develop a great love for the mountains. Decades later I, too, would buy a cabin in the mountains in Shaver Lake, 40 miles from Fresno.

When I had finally resolved in my young mind that Crestline was our new family home and I adjusted to life on the mountain, I loved to hike around the mountains by myself or walk down to the lake and fish with my handmade fishing-line-on-a-stick contraption. I don't even think my parents knew where I was half the time.

Sometimes, I got a little bored so I'd walk down to the macramé shop where they had an abundance of colorful yarn, and they taught me how to macramé. I asked the shop if I could work there but they said no since I was only nine. I was constantly looking for something to do and for ways to make money.

The first day of fourth grade arrived and I remember walking up to my new school, Valley of Enchantment Elementary School, and learning who my teacher was, Mr. Burke. I absolutely freaked out because I had never had a male teacher. I burst into tears. My mom reassured me, "Jill, it will be fine." Mr. Burke ended up being a great teacher and I came to like the small classes in this mountain town.

My brother was playing baseball and football and I started to play softball. Crestline had a Bonnet Ball team and my mom signed me up and that's really when I started to play softball. I played at first base and pitcher, which I liked, because it meant I was always actively involved in almost every play during games. I played softball during the remainder of my elementary and middle school years but stopped when I got to high school when volleyball and track became my focus.

It was funny because I'd be all into one sport, then we'd move and another sport would grab and hold my interest, or maybe a particular sport would be more popular and emphasized at another school. I don't recall why I ever stopped playing softball in high school—maybe it had something to do with the track coach—after all, I knew what a great coach was because of my dad.

Anyway, I ended up having male teachers in both fourth and fifth grade and yes, I was still challenging boys to foot races. There was this one boy who was really good friends with my brother and I boldly announced to him one day, "I think I can beat you in a race." He scoffed because he played football and baseball. We raced outside and I beat him. This guy was devastated and totally convinced that I had not beat him. But I did. Boys didn't like getting beat by girls then and they don't like it now either!

When Dad was coaching at UC Riverside, Crestline experienced the biggest snowstorm in their history. Our cars were buried under a heavy blanket of snow with absolutely no way to get out—a very frustrating situation for my mom. How my dad convinced my mom to live up in the mountains I will never know. My mom wasn't a person who wanted to be shoveling snow and maneuvering through snow and being isolated in the mountains. She was driving down to Riverside every day to take classes and the usual routine would be for her to take classes at every university where my dad coached, but this time she was actually attending a junior college because she hadn't finished up at San Jose State. My mom is a perpetual learner and I'm glad I've inherited that trait from her.

After we lived in Crestline for a while, my mom's dad moved up to Crestline. Grandpa was a writer and Hollywood agent after his punting days at Penn back in early 1919. His cousin, Pete, was also a Hollywood producer and worked with James Garner on several movies. Life in Crestline was great because now we had an abundance of family to visit and it was especially good for my mom because she was able to spend a lot of time with her dad. Now with family close by we would visit my grandpa every day.

One day at Grandpa's house, I had a brilliant idea: I'll build a lemonade stand and I'll sell lemonade right in front of Grandpa's house! He lived on the main drag and that meant that people who were out and about would stop by and buy a lemonade. A fine way to earn some extra cash.

I also thought it was an innovative idea to have a snow cone machine. Do you remember those snow cone machines that had the little crank on them? Maybe I'm dating myself but they were quite popular back then.

So I began my business making snow cones and lemonade. I don't know what I was charging, but again, it was simply something to do in the super small town we lived in; there was literally a grocery store and a few other shops and that was about it in Crestline, California.

Several of my parents' friends owned cabins in the area, including the Joneses. The Jones family would come up for a week or so during the summer—their cabin was not far from ours—and they belonged to a club at Lake Gregory. We often went with them to the club to play shuffleboard and volleyball and engage in all the different games and activities, which we loved. Now surrounded by family and visiting friends like the Joneses, I had learned to love the mountains even more.

But back to football…

During the season, my family would drive down to Riverside to go to the UC Riverside football games, especially now that they were winning. One of the players who played for my dad at UC Riverside was Russ Bollinger; he is like one of our family members. Russ ended up coaching for my dad and then he went into a long scouting career with the NFL. Russ has remained a constant friend throughout my life. One of my main mantras is if you're going to be in sports, you need connections. I was only nine when I met Russ so you can see how long and deep my connections run.

Years later, Russ was scouting in Fresno when my kids were in elementary school. Russ was on his way to stop by our ranch to visit and the girls were walking home from the bus. He pulled his car up beside them to see if they needed a ride but the girls hadn't met Russ yet so they refused to get in his car. We had always told them not to get in a car with a stranger no matter what they said. He told them, "I am friends with your parents." My girls still refused to get in his car. We all laugh about that story now but my girls stood their ground on that day.

Pat Hill was another player on UC Riverside's team. After I married, my husband would end up working for him at Fresno State and my husband and Pat coached together at the University of Arizona. Pat also coached with my dad at the University of Utah. So again, connections were made early on because they were all on the same staff together, or they played for my dad.

Interestingly enough, Wayne Howard's staff went from Gavilan Junior College to UC Riverside to Long Beach State, and then University of Utah. The entire staff moved together. So I was with the same group of people and coaches' kids from the time I was five or six years old through college. Many of those same people who were on coach Howard's staff coached with my dad.

The coaching staffs were very cohesive—people didn't leave. My mom still talks about when my dad got a job offer at UCLA and he didn't take it because he thought that meant he would be disloyal to Wayne Howard. Unlike today, loyalty was really important, and my dad liked working for Wayne Howard. Every decision they made was centered around football, a football season, or a football game.

My entire life even now revolves around a football season, a football game, a football player, or a football coach—and I'm a sports agent—so it's engrained in every fiber of my being. And that's also why it's so easy for me to be a sports agent because I just understand the industry. I understand every aspect of it because I grew up in and around it.

When you've been in the sports world as long as I have you're bound to collect stories…lots of them! I think many people wonder how a female sports agent operates in a man's world. At my parents' house, we never even talked about that type of stuff—you got your work done and that's what you were supposed to do. Period.

In the midst of growing up I was exposed to a lot of things that probably most other kids weren't exposed to because of my dad. For instance, my dad took us with him all the time to his various meetings and social gatherings, and sometimes his friends were just a little bit nuts. One story in particular stands out.

I don't recall why we were with my dad that day, but he took us to a rugby game because he was playing and all of his college friends who, by the way, ended up coaching with him, were also playing in this rugby game. My mom wasn't there, but my brother, sister and I were with him at the game. The team Dad was playing with must have won because afterward he and his rugby buddies decided to stop for pizza. We all went into the pizza place; keep in mind that my dad friends' idea of fun might differ from most people.

I didn't know this at the time but one of his friends, a guy by the name of Wayne Hogue, who also coached with my dad all the way through the University of Utah, ate glass. Another friend who was there, Sterk the Jerk, well, he ate watches. You read that correctly. Yes, these guys ate glass and watches…for fun.

So we were in the pizza parlor and these guys had had a few beers and they decided to bet somebody who worked at the pizza parlor that Sterk the Jerk would eat his watch in exchange for free pizza and beer. Amazingly, the pizza place employee takes the bet. Now, not only is Sterk the Jerk eating the employee's watch, Wayne is eating glass at the same time. The people seated at other tables and the employee are staring with their mouths open and eyes as wide as saucers as gasps echoed around the room.

My dad's group were by now getting kind of out of control and some sort of confrontation occurred. The police were called. My dad told us kids, "All right now let's all run to the car!" All of us sprinted out to the car and as soon as he got in the car Dad said, "Okay now, don't tell your mother about what happened at the pizza place."

I'm mortified at this point at what has unfolded before my eyes, or maybe I was just scared because these guys were eating glass and watches and obviously drinking too much beer. But we did get away. Apparently, the cops did not get there and we were able to get home without being confronted (or arrested) on the glass and watch eating.

When we got home my brother, sister, and I immediately told my mother what had happened although she was not surprised about Sterk the Jerk. She knew the stories. She already knew that he would probably have too much to drink and then eat a watch. Dad's common theme "don't tell your mom" was because my mom would get pissed off and ask, "Why are you putting our children in a vulnerable position by taking them with you to the pizza parlor when you know some of your friends might get crazy?"

The truth is my dad knew his buddies' tendencies and that they had done this stuff before, but I don't think he thought it would happen at a family pizza place.

***

Wayne Howard was very successful at UC Riverside and he ended up getting the head coaching job at Long Beach State and he hired my dad to coach with him which would mean another move for the McBrides and a major change of scenery from living in the mountains to relocating to Huntington Beach, California.

We moved to a rental house in Huntington Beach because my parents wanted us to go to Edison High School although at the time I was still in middle school. We lived in a rental house for one year until my parents bought a house in Huntington Beach and we moved again. So she had the job of moving us twice in a single year. The house they bought was across the street from the middle school we were attending and in the Edison High School District. Again my mother made these major life transitions look really easy.

This was back when schools didn't pay for coaches to move. I'm pretty sure my mom had to figure out how she was going to move from the rental to the Huntington Beach house, and I don't recall if my dad helped or not. He rounded up some players to help with the actual move and they did the heavy lifting because obviously we couldn't pick up all that furniture and move it.

And here we were, back to having strangers living at our house.

One day a guy, must have been a player, came to stay at our house and he took over my bedroom so I had to vacate and sleep somewhere else in the house. I don't exactly know why he ended up staying at our house but I didn't like this guy from day one. I thought he was a creep, and now he was staying in my room. Of course all my personal belongings were in there so I started snooping around this guy's stuff and found that he had some really strange letters from people. It seemed like he was pissing a lot of people off.

Well, come to find out, this guy robbed our neighbors, he was the supermarket bandit, and later on he finally ended up in prison. I knew he was a bad person from the start and all kinds of bad things happened while he was staying at our house.

My parents were just so trusting, especially if they thought somebody was down and out—they were always trying to help somebody out with something.

Our house also had a lot of stuff stored in the garage. A piano was one of those items. Turns out, a guy by the name of Joe Paopao, a great quarterback who played for my dad at Long Beach State, loved to play the piano. He'd come over just to play that darned piano in the garage. This was our "normal."

Not surprisingly, Wayne and my dad were very successful at Long Beach State. I really liked summers there because my dad would sign us kids up for camp, and besides all the other fun activities, the camp included a really fun 49ers camp. We took swimming lessons and learned to play racquetball. There was archery, basketball, volleyball, gymnastics and track and I think we learned to sail too.

At this particular camp, I was just crushing everybody in my group so I talked to my dad. "I don't know what's going on but these kids just don't seem to be able to keep up with what's going on." My dad, not remembering how old I was, had put me in an age group that was about two or three years off from where I should have been. So once I got in the right age group things were much better and I was better matched ability-wise.

What was great about being a coach's kid was that we were exposed to so many different athletic events and a wide variety of coaches who were extremely adept at their skill. For someone like me who really loves sports, I learned a little bit about every sport and then figured out which ones I liked the best.

Alternatives to Playing Football

Since I couldn't play on the football team I became a cheerleader for my brother's fourth grade flag football team, and I remember getting very annoyed when the other cheerleaders did not know what a first down was or how many yards a team had to go to get a first down. That meant they didn't know what cheer to do at the right time and I admit that really irritated me to no end.

I ended up cheerleading all the way through high school in addition to whatever sport I was playing in any given season. Back then you could do everything. It's interesting because I played volleyball, I ran track, I was on the drill team, I was a cheerleader, and I was on the dance team. In that era, you didn't have to just stick to one thing—you could do five or six things—and that was fine with me...still is!

Chapter 2

Law School and Decision to Become a Sports Attorney

Tragedy can strike no matter how young or old you are, no matter your socio-economic background, no matter what ethnicity you are—it can happen in an instant. For my family and me, it happened when I was in eighth grade.

My mom's brother was an attorney who worked at the Public Defender's office. He had remained friends with an ex-girlfriend. Well, the ex had gotten involved with a very bad person; an old boyfriend from high school who had always been obsessed with her. She had asked this former boyfriend to come get her from whatever state she was living in and bring her back to California.

Once she was back in California she immediately broke up with him because she basically just used him to get herself moved.

Unfortunately, he turned out to be a stalker and not mentally dialed in properly. She called my uncle and asked if she could stay at his house because she was really scared and concerned about the situation with this mentally unstable guy. My uncle, who lived in Palm Springs at that time, said yes. He had a new girlfriend and I think she was living there too.

Once she was staying at my uncle's house, the crazy ex-boyfriend started making threatening phone calls to my uncle. The man eventually went to his house and, as my uncle was getting out of his car, the man fatally shot him, went inside the house, kidnapped his ex-girlfriend, threw her in his car, and then set my uncle's house on fire. The crazy ex drove to Mexico, and once they got there she pretended to be sick and went to a doctor. That's how they captured this guy.

My mom got that fateful call in the middle of the night when my dad wasn't home. She was absolutely hysterical because this was her only brother, and we were super close to him.

My uncle's murder was what really motivated me to become an attorney—I wanted to make sure this didn't happen to anybody else. He was the kindest person in the world and wouldn't hurt a fly.

School Days and Move Days

At the time, I was very involved at my middle school in Huntington Beach, Gisler Junior High. I cheered, did gymnastics, and was in the school play. I don't think they had a track team, so I didn't run track, but I played softball. I really enjoyed playing all those sports and being active in my school.

Not long after my uncle's death, our lives again took another dramatic turn. Wayne Howard's success at Long Beach State led to another offer to become head job at the University of Utah. At this point, my dad had been Coach Howard's line coach and offensive coordinator, moving with him when schools called: Gavilan Junior, UC Riverside, and then Long Beach State. Now he was being asked to move to Utah.

Of course, my parents had just been dealt the tragic blow of my uncle's murder, and now my mother was once again being asked to move and to sell our house in Huntington Beach. I was very involved in sports and other activities; entrenched with my friends and really having a great experience in middle school in Huntington Beach, nicknamed Surf City, which was known as one of the greatest surfing destinations in the world. My brother, who was in his freshman year at Edison High School, was wrestling and playing football. My sister, who was in elementary school, really liked Huntington Beach as well.

I can't imagine how my mom must have felt having to move at that time. Her dad moved to Long Beach from Crestline, which was close by, so Mom was having to leave her own parents at a time when they all really needed each other. That was a pretty hard time for my mom, and really for all of us.

When we got to Salt Lake City, we lived in the dorms. My mom decided that we were going to build a house so we stayed in temporary housing during the process. She met with a builder because she wanted us to be in a certain school district so we could go to Skyline High School. She bought a lot in the Holladay area just outside Salt Lake City and built a house there. My mom continued to make everything look easy to us even though it had to have been a difficult time for her.

We lived in the dorms in typical McBride fashion—we only had three rooms and one bathroom. I don't recall if we had a small kitchen or not, but the lack of space did not deter us from welcoming the Chaid family during that summer.

Dave Chaid had played football with my dad and had brought his wife and sons Danny and Steven to visit. We welcomed this family of four with open arms and the best thing was that all of us kids ran all over campus and did whatever we wanted to do.

Our relationship with the Chaids would help me later in life. Danny Chaid was a fantastic wrestler who wrestled very successfully in college. Later, after my husband John and I were married, and while my husband coached at the University of Maryland, Danny was trying to make the Olympic wrestling team and was staying at the du Pont Estate with the other national wrestlers. The Estate was only a few hours away so Danny went to the Penn State game with me. Fortunately for Danny, he and his wife left the estate right before his best friend, gold-medal wrestler David Schultz, was killed by the mentally ill du Pont heir, John du Pont, in 1996. The movie Foxcatcher depicts the gruesome story.

Later on when I was going to represent a UFC fighter, I called Danny to ask him about the best training for wrestling because UFC fighters wrestle and perform jujitsu and he offered some very helpful advice. The connections I made early on in my life often helped me in my career and that's why it's important to nurture strong relationships throughout your life. You never know who is going to be able to help you, and when you'll be able to do likewise.

Utah became one of my parents' favorite places to live, and they still live there to this day. But it was a difficult time of transition for me. I had just graduated from eighth grade and was supposed to move on to high school but in Salt Lake I had to go back to junior high for ninth grade, and I didn't really like that much. They decided that my brother should take a year off because he had always been young for his grade, so he was home for the first semester of school.

We moved out of the dorms because school was about to start, and the house wasn't done, so we had to stay with one of the other coaches, Wayne "Jugi" Hogue, his wife Clara, and their three boys for a couple of weeks. "Jugi" had also coached with Wayne Howard and had played rugby with my dad in San Jose, and Clara was one of my mom's best friends.

The coaching families always helped each other out. I grew up with that example—if somebody needed a place to stay for some reason, they always ended up with my parents. And after we married, John and I carried on that same philosophy. Any time somebody needed a place to stay, they would come to our house—I can think of four different people who have lived with us when they were transitioning from one place to another, and I will add that we always enjoy the company. It can be a lot during game week to have company, especially if it's compounded with losing a game.

***

My first day at Churchill Junior High will go down in my memory as…well…not so good. I had forgotten my lunch so my mom dropped my lunch off at the school office but I never got it. Another student took my lunch so I came home that first day starving and really upset. I didn't know anybody and I had no lunch because another student had stolen it.

My mom, who as you know by now is quite feisty, got mad at my dad over the lunch incident and marched over to practice and in no uncertain terms told him, "I can't believe you moved us to a place where students take other students' lunches!"

One of the players at practice overheard my mother, and it turned out that his girlfriend's sister was in my class in ninth grade at Churchill Junior High.

My second day of school the player's girlfriend's sister, Wendy, came up to me and introduced herself. Wendy was one of the first people I met, and she introduced me to three other great young women. That's all it took—I immediately tried out for volleyball and also signed up to run for office. I don't think track had started yet, but the point is I was involved and came home that second day as happy as a clam. The first day I came home utterly upset and the second day I was completely fine.

It would be many years later that the same scenario would play out in my own kids' lives. They would both become hysterical, telling us that we were the worst parents because we were moving them to a new place. I'd call John and say, "Well, apparently we're bad parents and the kids are upset because we're moving them."

I learned so much from my own childhood experiences which would later translate into my own parenting. Ultimately, I came to the same conclusion my parents had; I loved living in Utah. At Churchill Junior High, I played every available sport including volleyball and track because they had a great track team and coach. We even had half a day a week when we went skiing and received ski lessons. That year I was named the best female athlete of the school. I even got a job babysitting every week for the PE coach who had three little boys; I babysat by playing baseball with them in the backyard.

One of the more interesting things about Salt Lake City is there is one dominant religion there, Mormonism, although in our household, the religion was football.

Somebody asked me when we first moved to Utah, "Are you a member of the church?"

I was like, "What church?"

I really didn't know. I came home and asked my parents. "The kids keep talking about some church. What are they talking about?"

My mom said, "Oh, don't worry about it; just go down to the ward and play volleyball."

Now, ward was what they called the different districts, and each area had a church right down the street. None of us became Mormon. The kids we played sports with and their families all wanted us to convert to their religion but the only thing we ever did was invite in the missionaries and listen to their thoughts and that was fine. I would sometimes go to different events with my Mormon friends, and I have to say a lot of my friends are Mormon and they're great people. When I first came to Salt Lake, I was a little shocked that almost everyone shared the same religion. I hadn't really lived anyplace where there was one dominant religion, and growing up in our family, nobody followed any religion.

At Skyline High School, I would experience for the first time the big rivalry between Utah and BYU football. A lot of kids had an opinion about the game, and the BYU fans were always hoping every week that my dad was going to lose. If they were Utah fans, of course, they wanted Utah to win, but they always had an opinion about how the game went, and, of course, I went to every game, so I argued with all kinds of people all day long and defended my dad. After a while I think they just chose not to say much to me because they weren't going to win anyway, and my guess is that I probably scared them.

Nonetheless I had a great experience at high school in Utah. Our volleyball team ended up winning the state championship. I was a setter, which I loved, because I got to touch the ball on every single play. I also was head cheerleader during my senior year. Luckily, I could play at my volleyball game and then go to the football game and cheer.

In addition to that I ran track while I was in high school, and practice started on the first day of school. I had a great track coach, Craig Poole, who trained the boys team and the girls team together. He wanted to make sure that I was going to run track because he had heard from the middle school coach that I was fast. On the track team I ran hurdles and long-jumped and high-jumped. He made us run the mile relay, which was so hard after a track meet, but he wanted us to stay in shape. He later became the track coach at BYU. Simultaneously, I started track practice, volleyball practice, and cheer. I don't know how I managed all that but I did.

During my junior year of high school I was actually on the drill team and on the dance team and competed in track and volleyball.

After I graduated from high school I really wanted to go away to college. I truthfully didn't want to attend the University of Utah but my parents got half off tuition there, so they said, "That's where you're going." And that's where I went.

There were three of us in college at the same time: my brother, me, and my mom, who had started taking classes again. With the three of us attending the University of Utah at the same time, my parents were up to their eyeballs paying tuition.

I was always a really good student, very motivated, and I really wanted to go to UCLA or the University of Colorado at Boulder. I don't think I really thought about Berkeley, but I liked UCLA and their colors. I thought, wow, they're a big football school, and my mom grew up nearby in Santa Monica so that would be perfect.

The connection was being formed even then for my future: My mom is a brilliant person. Her dad, my grandpa, was an agent/writer in the movie business. My dad is an exceptionally good coach. My uncle who was killed was an attorney, and, interestingly enough, I chose to become a sports agent. It all fits together!

My dad and my mom both encouraged us to get involved in all kinds of activities and sports. Anytime we found out about a new sport my dad and I usually learned it together. As I mentioned earlier, we got into windsurfing—probably when I was in college—my dad and I would take off with the windsurfer on the car. If it was just the two of us we would forget to bring food and water, and probably didn't have the windsurfer attached to the roof very well. But off we'd go on our adventures. My dad didn't really pay attention to what I was doing so I could be out in the middle of the lake, and he would assume I was fine and that I could figure it out, which is why I really loved windsurfing. We got ourselves into a few pickles when it was a little too windy, but we had a lot of fun.

High school ended and I moved on to the University of Utah but in my second year there, my dad got offered another job. Wayne Howard quit as the head coach. My dad was turned down for the head coaching job so he stayed there for another season and worked for the head coach they hired, Chuck Stobart. I don't think my dad was too fond of his philosophy because it was completely different from Wayne Howard's. When my dad got offered a job at the University of Wisconsin, he decided it was time to go.

My mom decided to keep the house in Salt Lake and rent it out when they moved to Wisconsin. I stayed in Utah. My parents told my sister who was then a senior, "Well, you can stay behind with Jill," but my sister said, "No way, she's going to be stricter than you are," which was probably true. My siblings and I never did anything wrong because we knew not to mess with our parents, although they didn't have many rules. Truth is they had three: be nice to everybody, don't lie, and don't ride an ATV or motorcycle. (My sister actually did ride a motorcycle one time, and, of course, she got in an accident.)

Those were the three McBride team rules of the house and that was it. Otherwise, my parents just let us make our own decisions, and we knew when something was not a good idea, so we just didn't do it.

We had really great parents and it was my mother in particular who really instilled good values and good decision-making skills because she allowed us to make decisions. We learned from the good and bad decisions we made.

In college I worked in the football office, and, if you're wondering if I dated football players, yes, I did. I went out with one guy who was on the football team at the University of Utah for four years. I remember walking into my dad's office and telling him, "Oh, yeah, I'm dating one of the players." I don't recall what he said exactly, but he probably said, "I don't know if that's a good idea, Jill."

But you live and learn. Back in the '80s, players were pretty wild. And my dad probably knew that, probably didn't like the idea that I was dating one of the defensive linemen. I'm still great friends with him to this day and all of his friends, because we all had the same friends in college. And my brother was just a year ahead of me; I knew all of his friends and we all lived in the dorms together.

When you're in college and your dad is coaching there, and you're at parties where there are players who maybe like the coach or maybe don't, you hear all the chatter about the sports politics. It was a little harder as a coach's kid to listen to players make less than admiring comments about the coach.

Luckily, my dad was the kind of coach the players liked, so they usually didn't say anything about him. But they might say unfavorable things about another coach, and I remember being ultra-sensitive to negative remarks because I just didn't like them talking bad about other coaches.

Also, sometimes players did not behave themselves. I remember once that somebody stole a van from the Marriott and put it on another player's lawn. They were always getting into fights at the fraternity and the police would be called. But that was back then—now those same guys would have lost their scholarships and been kicked off the team. Plus, there was no social media back then and that's probably a very good thing with the antics some of the players were involved in.

Even though my parents couldn't afford for us to go away to college, they said we could live in the dorms if we went to the University of Utah. I lived at Van Cott Hall. My brother also lived in the dorms so we saw each other all the time and we shared a car.

At college, I joined a sorority and became a Delta Gamma. It proved to be a great organization over the years to come because it was national. Later in life after I married a coach, every time we moved, I would affiliate immediately with the local Delta Gamma sorority so that I could get to know the alumni in the area.

Now I am an advisor for the Delta Gammas at USC, and I was an advisor for them at the University of Michigan when we lived there. I still enjoy being around college-age kids and helping them.

The other sport I was really into while in college was racquetball. I played intramural softball with all of the Greek row and I believe we had a volleyball team too. I was always involved in intramural sports throughout my college career.

But back to my parents' move to Wisconsin. When they left me behind in Salt Lake, it was the first time I'd really been away from my family. My brother Mike couldn't handle my parents being away so he decided to move with them and transferred to the University of Wisconsin.

I stayed back at the University of Utah, but the University of Wisconsin Badgers ended up going to the Hall of Fame Classic in 1984 so I traveled to Wisconsin so I could fly on the team charter flight with my family to Birmingham for the bowl game, and while I was there I met people who later became NFL football scouts.

One of the coaches' kids on the Wisconsin staff went on to become a scout, and I still run into him from time to time. Because we were around football, many coaches' kids went into coaching or found some other profession close to the game.

Ted Tollner's son Bruce, who's a good friend to me now, became an agent. His dad and my dad were never on the same staff; they played against each other, but my parents were great friends with Ted and his wife Barbara. The Tollners are a wonderful family. When Bruce, their son, became an agent, I started to get to know him, and then our daughters ended up going to college together at the University of Washington. This business really is a fish bowl; you tend to run into the same people over and over.

Coach Ted Tollner went to Cal Poly, San Luis Obispo, and went to college with my dad's cousin Kathy and her husband Roy. Roy and Ted played football at Cal Poly. They were on the flight that crashed on the way home from an away game. My dad's cousin Dick ended up pulling—I think it was Ted—out of the plane. Roy also survived the crash. If you go into the Coliseum at USC you will see their names on a plaque called the Mercy Bowl. It was a game after the crash. Oddly enough that's where my husband coaches now. If that hadn't happened, Ted probably wouldn't be here right now.

I just find it weird how we were all connected through football and how each of them continues to circle through my life.

As a coach's kid I came to recognize the importance of relationships. Many players who my dad coached later became coaches in the NFL and college. Thanks to my parents and their open door, I was really well connected in the sports industry before I ever started law school.

After my undergraduate years, I went to law school. I didn't get too involved during my first year but all that changed during my second year. I became president of the sports law forum and president of the women's caucus, and I was also a community legal services attorney on campus, which meant I was helping indigent clients with various legal issues.

Law school was very difficult and a grind. I grew up in sports, so immediately when I got into law school, I started to participate in intramural sports. We had co-ed football, a flag football team, a co-ed volleyball team and a co-ed softball team at law school, and I was on all those teams, which I really enjoyed. One of my other law school friends was a rugby player, so we used to watch him play rugby between studying. Beyond sports, my daily routine consisted of getting up in the morning, attending class, studying all day, studying all night. I got up each day and repeated the process. I did that for three years.

I worked the entire time I was in college; I worked in the football office, at the bookstore, at Nordstrom's in the sports department, and I waitressed. I always had a part-time job. I can't recall a time during college that I ever didn't have a job.

Even in high school I worked at a pizza place during the school year, and then during summers, I worked at the sports mall and cleaned the bathrooms. And it wasn't like my parents said that I had to get a job. I just always wanted to work.

I was going to law school in northern California, and, during my second year there, sports agent Lee Steinberg came to speak to our entire student body. I remember raising my hand and asking, "Do you think there could be any female sports agents?" And he said, "No."

Little did he know what was about to happen. About two weeks later, my dad called me and said, "Hey, Gary (one of his players) needs help. Can you figure out what you have to do to help him? He's getting a contract offer from the Rams and he needs an agent."

So I called Lee Steinberg's office and he referred me to a guy by the name of Steve Baker, with whom I'm still friends to this day.

I said, "Hey, Steve, what do I have to do to become a sports agent?"

He said, "Well, you just have to get registered with the NFLPA and pay the money and you'll be a sports agent."

So that's what I did. And I negotiated my first contract for Gary Anderson, who is now the head coach at Utah State. He's also been the head coach at Oregon State and at the University of Wisconsin. But Gary also played for my dad at the University of Utah and he and I went to college together although I was older than him. I'm still friends with Gary, and now I represent a coach on his staff and always track to see what kind of players he has in his roster, as like my dad, Gary is a good recruiter. The way this business works is relying on knowing people and developing strong relationships.

I was working with the community legal services when I helped Gary with his contract. I didn't have files yet so I took detailed notes on everything that happened with Gary. I kept a log of every phone call I made, every person I talked to.

Back then, I actually negotiated the deal with a guy by the name of Hudson Houck, who was an offensive line coach, and a guy named Dick Coury. Now there are a lot more front office people than there were back then, so there would be more people involved.

Once I went to a meeting for the NFL Players Union and I got to know a guy by the name of Mike Duberstein, a really fascinating guy. He was the one who had done all the work with sharing salary information with everyone who was certified with the union. He was the one who created all of the stats and kept track of everything—he was a brilliant guy. He was the salary cap guy for many, many years for the union.

Mark Levin, who still works for the Players Union, was an intern back then. Now, he is in charge of everything that has to do with salary caps. I first got certified as an NFL player union in 1987, and we had to attend regular meetings and that's when I met all these great men. There weren't that many who attended those early meetings but I remember going to my first meeting when I was in law school, I'm thinking it was in Los Angeles. I was the only woman registered as an agent with the Union, I just didn't know it at the time. The other attendees were welcoming and very helpful.

I remained the only woman in the Union for a long time. There weren't even that many sports agents at the time because a lot of players weren't represented back then. Now everybody is represented. The coaches weren't being represented either, and that has completely changed, which I'll talk about later in the book.

After I graduated from law school, I went to work for an insurance defense law firm in Southern California. I absolutely hated it!

I moved to Arizona where my parents lived, and got a job at the DA's office, took the Bar there in Arizona and passed. I decided that as long as I was studying for the Bar in Arizona, I'd study for the Utah Bar too and became licensed in two states.

I was living in Arizona while my dad was coaching at U of A, so I decided to live with my parents. After two tries, my dad finally got the head coaching job there—becoming a head coach had been a circuitous path for him. After my dad went to Wisconsin, he returned to Utah to work for Jim Fassel. (Jim's son, who is my friend now, currently coaches for the Rams.) Dad worked for Jim for a year, and then Dick Tomey got the head coaching job in Arizona and hired my dad to be his offensive line coach and offensive coordinator. That's why I ended up moving to Arizona. My dad worked for Coach Tomey, who ended up being one of my biggest mentors.

At that time, my husband, John Baxter, (before we were married) was on the staff at the University of Arizona (U of A). John was a GA (Graduate Assistant) for special teams while my dad was the offensive line coach. So he, Tim Davis and Rob Bernardi were GAs together. Again, it's all about those relationships. Rob later went on to become an AD, and his brother ended up playing for us at Fresno State.

Chapter 3

Marriage and Kids

After I moved to Arizona, John went to the University of Maine in his first full-time job as a GA. My dad applied for the head coaching job at the University of Utah because Jim Fassel got fired. They hired my dad that time around to be the head coach. My dad tried to employ John Baxter as his special teams coordinator or for some position on his staff. But Coach Tomey had an opening on his staff and asked John to come back as a special teams coordinator and tight end coach. Coach Tomey also offered Pat Hill the offensive line job to take over for what my dad was doing. Pat had been at Fresno State as an offensive line coach with Jim Sweeney. (Pat played for my dad at UC Riverside, and I had known him since I was about eight years old.)

John decided to go back to U of A. At the time I was trying to figure out who could get me tickets to games. John was the only one on the staff who was single, so I approached him and said, "Hey, can I get tickets to the game from you?" He said, "Sure."

I was living with my friend Mary Ann Hassey, whose brother, Ron Hassey, played baseball. One year we traveled to the World Series when Ronnie was catching for the Oakland A's. Mary Ann and I played golf and racquetball together. We played in tournaments and we're still friends to this day. She is a teacher in Tucson now.

Mary Ann was dating a guy by the name of John at the time, and I told her one day, "Well, let's invite John Baxter over, and we'll cook dinner and watch a movie with them." So we did that. Well, we burned the dinner, and it was a terrible movie. But that's how I started to date John—although I don't think he thought it was a date. In fact, one time he saw me at Tucson Racquet Club and said, "Hey, Kelly." That's my sister's name, so he wasn't even sure about my name. It's funny how things work out.

On my first actual date with John, he took me to a neighbor's house for dinner. I should have realized then that this guy was not a dater. He didn't like to date. He still doesn't enjoy going out to dinner. So we went over to Fred and Edith's, who lived next door to him and are still good friends, and then went back to his house to watch When Harry Met Sally.

Fred was an attorney in Tucson, and Edith was a paralegal. John was super close to Fred and to their kids. Every time we go to Arizona we stop by to visit with Fred, Edith, and their son, Joe. Their daughter is married and lives in Phoenix.

After John and I started dating seriously, one day I asked, "Have you ever been to Vegas?" He hadn't. That's when I realized this guy had not dated very much and he was pretty naïve. So I took him to Vegas a couple of months after we started dating; it was around St. Patrick's Day. And he was like, "Maybe we should just get married." I said, "No, I think maybe my parents would want to go to the wedding."

A year later John was offered the job at the University of Maryland under Head Coach Mark Duffner. Arizona had had a bad year, and Pat Hill and John both ended up leaving. Pat went to work for Bill Belichick at the Cleveland Browns, and John got a position working for Mark Duffner at Maryland.

That job offer came in January, and he didn't know whether to take it or not. At this point, I was working at the DA's office prosecuting criminals and really liked my job. I rode my bike to work, played racquetball after work, learned how to play golf, and played in a volleyball league.

When John decided to go to Maryland, I said, "Well, what do you want to do? Do you want to get married or break up?"

He replied, "Well, I guess we'll get married." So we called my parents and told them the news. Our wedding date was in two months because we wanted to get married on St. Patrick's Day during John's spring break. (My parents were married on St. Patrick's Day, too)

So I gave notice at my job at the DA's office, and we got married in Salt Lake, where my dad was now the head coach. My mom and my sister planned the wedding. John and I literally just showed up.

A day before John and I got married, the guy my dad played racquetball with, who was a priest, asked me, "Hmm, have you been baptized?"

"Nope, I've never been baptized."

He absolutely freaked out. He said, "I'm just going to pretend I never heard that."

His parish was at the Holy Cross Hospital in Salt Lake, so the chapel wasn't going to be big enough for us to get married in, but he agreed to marry us anyway. My husband is Catholic, so it was important to him.

We went skiing the day before the ceremony and good thing we both came back with no limbs broken, all in one piece—we didn't expect anything different. We went to an Irish pub for our rehearsal dinner, which seemed fitting for our Irish heritage. We got married downstairs in the atrium at the Utah Park Hotel where Rick Majerus happened to live.

On the day of my wedding, my dad scheduled a clinic. He wanted my very-soon-to-be husband to train the guys on special teams…the day of my wedding. My mom got mad that my dad would schedule anything on that day but all the while I didn't know any of this was going on.

And did I tell you that I bought my own wedding ring? He still hasn't paid me for the wedding ring. After 25 years, I'm still waiting…

It was snowing on the day of our wedding, on a Wednesday in the middle of the week. So two things happened on my wedding day: One, since my dad had scheduled the clinic, he and John barely made it in time for the wedding. My mother was very pissed off and it was no doubt a continuation of her being mad at Dad for even scheduling a clinic in the first place. And two, as my dad was just about to walk me down the aisle he saw Rick Majerus, the University of Utah head basketball coach at the time. He was like, "Hey, what's going on?" Lucky for me, they didn't converse for too long.

Rick actually lived in the hotel, and there was my dad having his daughter's wedding where Rick lived. (Rick never had his own place; he lived in the Utah Park Hotel the whole time he was the head basketball coach at the University of Utah, and he and my dad were great friends. He was a great basketball coach.)

My dad did another interesting thing for my wedding. It was spring break for the players, so technically they could work. So, unbeknownst to my mother, he fired all the bartenders right before the wedding and hired a few football players to tend bar so they could make money. I don't quite know what the outcome was, or when my mom found out, but I guess it turned out okay.

My mom was a saint but my dad was always doing crazy stuff. I don't know how my mom managed it all. It was a lot easier to be a coach's kid than a coach's wife because this kind of crazy stuff happened all the time. I'm sure my mom has more stories that I don't even know about.

Through the years I've learned so much about the importance of relationships, which is really why I'm sharing these story snippets with you. The people you meet throughout your life, especially in the sports world, tend to cross paths in one way or another, so fostering strong relationships is essential.

To illustrate my point, one of the assistant coaches on Rick's staff, Kerry Rupp, later became a client of mine. He's now the associate head basketball coach at Oregon State. He was a basketball coach for Rick Majerus back when my dad was the head coach at the University of Utah. It's like this colorful thread called relationships weaves itself in, around, and through every person I have ever met, and continue to meet.

After John and I got married, we didn't have a honeymoon. I went back to Arizona to finish up my DA job, and he returned to his coaching position at Maryland. The night after our wedding we went to a Utah Jazz basketball game and then stayed at my parents' house. Never did go on a honeymoon—another big mistake.

I finally moved to Maryland sometime in May and started looking for a job as I prepared to take the Bar there. I really wanted to work for one of the senators. I went and talked to one of the senators that my dad was friends with, Orrin Hatch, but we didn't really click. At the time, the Clarence Thomas hearings were going on, and I was arguing with him about that, and we just did not align politically. Great guy but our political philosophies were different.

I was ultimately hired by the National Victims Center. They had a big project going on about sexual assault, so I was able to do some policy work there. And then I got offered a teaching job at the University of Maryland in the Criminal Justice Department, which actually was a great job.

As a coach's kid, the few game losses we endured were bad but not the end of the world. As a coach's wife, what I didn't realize was that wins and losses are a lot more upsetting. My dad had never really had a losing season in his whole career. What he and his staff would do is take over a losing program and make it successful very quickly, and in that way they were always kind of the saviors, the underdogs that ended up winning. My dad was successful with Wayne Howard for so long, and then when my dad became a head coach his teams had winning records. My family had moved so Dad could take a better job, but he had never been fired.

When we lived in Maryland, John and I lived in a townhome. A freaky thing that happened was that a rapist was operating right in the area where we lived so we had to install a baby monitor even though we didn't have kids yet because this guy was breaking into all the townhomes. He was stalking women in the area, and he broke into one of female coach's homes. She was attacked and she was the one who got the man caught. It was a scary time until he was arrested.

In Maryland, I spent a lot of time with one of the other coaches' wives, Debbie Christensen, who's still my friend to this day. Her husband Clyde was our quarterbacks coach when John worked for Mark Duffner at the University of Maryland.

Debbie had three wonderful kids with whom I was close. She and I were both runners so we decided to run a marathon together. We trained every day when I wasn't teaching. I don't recall how we placed, but it was fun training together.

My best friend from my undergrad days at the University of Utah, Melinda, who was a United pilot, also lived in Virginia. After college, she had moved back there to the area of Virginia where she grew up so now my best friend and I lived close together which was wonderful. We used to talk on the phone all the time and we did a lot of fun things together. I also became good friends with her parents.

When you move around a lot, it's interesting how you end up reconnecting with friends because it seems like all of a sudden now you're living in the same area.

Unfortunately, we did not have a good team in Maryland. We lost so many games, and during John's second year of coaching, a kicker he recruited didn't qualify to get admitted right before the season. I don't know if John ended up being the fall guy or what, but he didn't have a kicker and he was a special teams coach, so at the end of the year he was fired.

My husband wasn't the only one who lost his job. Mark Duffner was losing and he fired three on the staff which maybe he thought would solve his problem—a lot of coaches have that mindset and maybe firing does solve the problem and then again, maybe not; it might seem like a good solution at the time but usually the team and staff problems run much deeper than what firing a few guys might fix. Coach Duffner also got fired not too long after that because the team still wasn't winning.

When I came home from work one day, and John told me the news, I was shocked. I had never experienced that as a coach's daughter. I had to figure out what to do. I sold the townhouse, and John received a job offer to work with Buddy Teevens at Tulane in New Orleans.

After I sold the townhome and finished teaching my classes, I drove our red van down to New Orleans by myself. I stopped to spend the night with my familiar long-time family friends, the Christensens, who were living near Clemson in South Carolina at the time. Clyde had left Maryland already and was coaching at Clemson. The same night I stopped to spend the night, Tony Dungy, who I believe was coaching for the Vikings at the time, well Tony and his wife happened to be staying at Clyde and Debbie's the same night I was there. The Dungys were really good friends with Clyde and Debbie. I have found that the most random encounters forge new relationships and this overnight stay was no exception.

The importance of relationships showed up again when we made the move to Tulane. The Athletics Director, Kevin White, had worked at the same two locations where John had been; Loras College in Iowa where John had attended, and the University of Maine when John was coaching there. Kevin had recommended John to their head coach, and John ended up getting hired as the Special Teams Coordinator.

I have to say we really had a fantastic time living in New Orleans. We were glad to leave Maryland as it had not been our favorite place to live, and overall we just had a bad experience.

Sports Law…Here I Come

During our transition to Tulane I would take on a player here or there who was referred to me and I stayed registered as a certified sports agent. One of my old clients—Wayne Lammle—said, "Hey, I really want to try to get on a team." He had gone up to the CFL and I had represented some guys up there.

I had always had more than one job so I would be an instructor somewhere, but I'd still represent clients if they called me and needed help. What usually happened is that a coach would call me and say, "Jill, this guy needs representation." I'd have one or two players at a time; I didn't really do it full-time.

I got certified in the CFL (Canadian Football League) too because there were a lot of Canadians at the University of Arizona and the University of Utah. My dad had a lot of Canadian players because he recruited in Canada at the University of Arizona and at the University of Utah.

When we got to Tulane, Kevin White connected me with Gary Roberts, who is a very well-known sports law professor, and I believe he was the Assistant Dean of Tulane Law School at the time. One of the instructors decided not to come and teach in the international graduate program, and they needed somebody to fill the spot ASAP. I happened to walk in and immediately got hired for a great teaching job at Tulane Law School, which was fabulous.

In the summer I ran the International Graduate Student Program for all the students who were in the master's program for international law. In the fall, I taught all the international graduate students in legal research and writing. In the spring, I recruited students from other countries and that meant a month-long trip to Europe in January, the same time span John was recruiting. Of course, we didn't have kids at this point so I had the freedom to travel. I went all over Europe by myself and spoke at different universities discussing our LLM program at Tulane. I went to France, to four different cities in Germany, Switzerland, Netherland, and Belgium.

We remained at Tulane for three years, and during that time is when I experienced a major shift in direction. My sports law career became my full-time job, and I switched up everything because we had kids now and I wasn't one who really liked having my kids stay with a babysitter.

Honey, the Kids are Here!

Kelly was born first. She was two weeks late so my doctor suggested being induced. It was pouring rain when I went to the downtown hospital in New Orleans. The hospital was packed, the maternity ward full. We were lined up on gurneys and the young woman next to me was having intense labor pains. I think this scared John. They decided to put me on a dark floor with no staff as they thought it would be a while before I would actually deliver. I arrived at 8 pm and didn't have Kelly until the next day at 11:59. So the labor and delivery took about 28 hours.

Where was John? Well, he went with me to the hospital. He went with me to the dark floor. When he found out the doctor thought I wouldn't deliver until the following day he went home. It was a scary night being in labor for the first time on a dark floor, alone.

John did come back the next day with my mom. Thank goodness my mom was there!!! I do remember that John was telling jokes during the delivery, and my mom told him, "Hey, hey, John, this is not the time to be telling jokes. This is not funny." I'm sure it was just his way of coping with the situation.

Kelly has been nothing short of extraordinary. During her school years, Kelly got straight A's, swam, and was on a cheer team that won a national competition.

Now, our daughter McKenzie's birth; that's a different story. John was in the garage engaged in some sort of project—I think he was painting the garage because we had just moved into a new house. I poked my head out of the door between the garage and the house and announced, "Gosh, I think I'm in labor." He responded, "Oh, no, you're fine." I said, "No, I really do think I am."

I went back in the house and waited…and waited…and waited… with labor pains. By the time we went to the hospital, it was eight o'clock at night and John told me on the way there, "Oh, you're probably going to have to go home." I said, "No, I think I'm going to have this baby."

Sure enough, I delivered her about four hours later. Good thing we left the house when we did. My husband was supposed to be the tough coach but he's standing next to me while I'm about to deliver, and he says, "I'm about to get sick; I'm going to pass out." I'm sitting there going, "Okay, I'm having a baby with no medication, and you're the one about to pass out? Please!" What a wimp, I thought. He was the worst coach in the delivery room…I mean he really sucked…but of course he doesn't want to hear that.

When McKenzie was born, we literally flipped a coin on her name. Heads, it was going to be one name; tails, it was going to be another name—either McKenzie or Molly. She ended up being McKenzie because that's the way the coin fell.

I will say now that John is the best dad in the world, but he was just terrible in the hospital. He would get so squirmy and could not handle the whole ordeal at all, but once they were here, he would not put those girls down.

Before McKenzie was born, we moved to Fresno State so John could coach for Pat Hill. We call her "lucky McKenzie" because ever since she was born we have had really great winning streaks in football. McKenzie is now 22 years old, and I don't recall many losing seasons since she was born. In fact, I can't think of one bad season during the time John worked for Pat Hill.

But John wasn't all football; he had, and still has, another side, a domesticated side, that loves household chores. Lucky for me!

Mr. Mom

John is actually the more domesticated one of the two of us. In fact, if we were to change roles, he would have been the perfect stay-at-home dad because he's super good at laundry. After we got married, he started telling me how he did laundry; he even took the time to explain to me his meticulous process for washing, drying, and folding. I think I might have looked at him a little sideways as I replied, "Yeah, that's not how my mom did it." My mom taught us how to do our own laundry when we were growing up but her only goal was for each of us to just get the job done. John, on the other hand, had a system. He could have written a book about the exact way to do laundry; precise and meticulous. I mean this guy had a stick he used to stir up water and soap, and he stirred again after he added bleach. I thought, this guy is a whack-a-doodle. He's worried about laundry.

My dad never did laundry nor was he ever worried about laundry or how to do it. I'm certain my father has not done very many loads of laundry.

After hearing John go on at length about how I needed to do laundry, I looked at him and said, "I won't be doing your laundry." And, guess what? I've never done his laundry. He does his own laundry, I do mine, and I trained the girls pretty early to do their own. They claim they were doing laundry and making eggs by age five; they're probably right on that one.

They also could do their own hair at an early age because I didn't do their hair either. John would be the one more worried about what their outfits looked like, and what their hair looked like…just like Mr. Mom.

And food. John loves food. I couldn't care less about food. If he is home, he cooks and he also loves going to the grocery store. I'll even say sometimes, "Okay, I'll go to the grocery store," but he tells me, "No, no, no, no; you're going to forget something." And I have to admit that a lot of times I do—I'll be in the store and think what did he want again? I'm simply not a big fan of domestic chores, nor am I a big fan of the grocery store or the kitchen or the stove. I can follow a recipe, but it takes a lot of time and I'm constantly thinking that I could be doing something else, like something outside. I could be on an adventure somewhere.

As my mom said, the first time I walked into the kitchen I had a big question mark on my face because even back then I did not like to be anywhere near a kitchen. I just liked being outside. I lived outside as a child and definitely continued to love being outdoors.

When we got to Fresno State, I started practicing sports law full time—I didn't want to have a babysitter, so that was the best job for me. I could begin negotiating a deal during their nap time, or, when they were at school, I could do all my work, and I would hire out chores that I didn't want to do like housecleaning. (I didn't do that either.) You were more likely to find me out fixing the pool or mowing the lawn than staying inside.

Life by Design

I designed my life to be able to work really hard but also have a lot of fun, a lot of freedom. I love to travel and I love new experiences. I think that's one of the things I like the most about sports law; I love going to the games. I love traveling to new cities, getting to know people's families. I really, really enjoy that part of the job. I enjoy getting to know all the different coaches on the teams, and seeing the scouts and coaches at practice, and then seeing them ten years later at a practice and finding out how their families are doing and asking about their kids. Again, it's the strong relationships you build that make you successful in this business. But who knew at the time that relationship building would include horses?

We lived at one house in Fresno for a little while, and then shortly after McKenzie was born, we found out she loved animals so John took her to the equestrian facility at Fresno State and that's where she fell in love with the horses. Seeing her love for horses, John and I agreed, "Okay, if we could get a place with property, what would it look like?"

That spring we wrote down a five-year plan that included a house with some property but it turns out that we found a house within the next six months. We later sold that first house in Fresno to my parents, and they, in turn, rented it out. We were so excited when we found a house that had a main house and a second house on five acres of land. I liked the second house because I could work from there and my employees could come in and work yet it was separated from the main house.

Back then everything was completed on paper and that meant every single sale had to be printed out; I had a full-time office assistant who took care of all of that for me and I also hired interns for the summer to help me with my sports law business and Academic Gameplan. Having two kids and with John's coaching schedule it was organized chaos many days.

I didn't want to have a babysitter or a nanny. John and I both wanted to be able to go to the kids' games; we wanted to be able to coach the soccer team if we could and take McKenzie to her barrel racing practices and events.

When we moved out to the property, the kids were starting elementary school, and I think Kelly was five and McKenzie was four. Really, it was just such a great life for all of us living on five acres. I'm not going to lie; it was a lot of work. We had grapevines, a soccer field, an almond orchard, a barn, and a pool. Only one thing was missing: we didn't have any animals yet.

One day one of the equestrian girls wanted to leave her horse at our place for the summer. There was a horse by the name of Scooter that couldn't really compete anymore; he was getting older but he needed a home. So Scooter became the very first horse we actually owned, and he was the best horse ever. We all took lessons on him. McKenzie loved that horse. After that, John, Kelly, and McKenzie started to collect animals. We would get one horse, then another horse.

There was a player who played for John, McKenna Sean "Bear" Pascoe, whose parents were ropers, and Bear was and still is a steer wrestler. Bear had a horse, Bo, and somehow we ended up with Bo too.

Then John started to buy chickens. He bought a rooster that would run around the coop and chase the girls and scare them—that rooster was just awful. I'm sure the girls thought their parents had gone mad by buying that rooster.

One time a booster put a calf underneath my husband's desk, which he brought home. I think it was done on purpose so John could bring that calf home. The girls bottle-fed the calf, and then ultimately lent the cow to the dairy farm at Fresno State. We later sold it, and the money went into their college fund. We also bought some cows to put out on pasture that we later sold to put toward their college fund as well.

Now, we had animals and lots of them! At one point, we had chickens, ducks, goats, two or three horses, two dogs, two cats, along with two kids and two employees. To say it was a zoo at our house would be an understatement. And I was running two companies; my sports agent business and helping John with Academic Gameplan, an educational video series for kids.

John has always been a big advocate for helping kids learn. He'd always had an active game plan for how to put it all together, but he didn't have it in any form he could share with other people. Before we moved out to the bigger property, we spent a summer shooting an entire eight-hour video series teaching kids how to learn. In 1999, we created a workbook, planners and notebooks with the intention of sharing them with the world…and that's exactly what we did. After we shot all the videos, I found myself sitting in a dark room with a video editor, editing all this tape, which I had never done before. Back then it was all recorded on VHS.

After we created this incredible package of products, we began selling it to parents and also doing seminars. We started out with partners and then bought them out because we were doing all the work anyway.

Now, 20 years later, everything is online now, and I am still selling these educational packages on top of my sports law business. At this point I delegate a lot of the tasks for the educational packages and we are no longer conducting seminars.

Chapter 4

My Clients – It's All About Relationships

Marlon Moore is a client with whom I had a long long-term relationship. He was a wide receiver who played at Fresno State. During his sophomore year of college, his dad passed away, and he was very close to his dad, so it was a very difficult time for Marlon. He also had what I believe was a high ankle injury in his junior year but he came back and had a pretty good season during his senior year, which is when I met with Marlon and his mom.

I waited until after the season and the bowl game to meet with players. I didn't pursue them; they usually came to me. I frequently went to practice with my own kids, we typically had John's position players over a couple times a year, and I went to games. That's part of being a coach's wife. So I got to know the players and their parents and families pretty well from going to practice and attending all the games, including some of the away games.

Marlon had great speed and really knew how to leverage a play. I knew Marlon's talents and I wanted to get him on the right team. He was signed as an undrafted free agent with the Miami Dolphins. I can't recall what his initial choices were, but I felt Miami was a really good place for him to go—it turned out to be a great team for him.

Part of my job was to analyze the other wide receivers on the team to discern who their second and third guys were and then figure out if Marlon had the talent to beat those guys out for a spot. And he did. He made the 53-man roster in Miami his very first year. He was maybe the third or fourth wideout on the depth chart, so he usually saw some action during a game, especially during certain plays. He played for the Dolphins with his first contract the whole time, and then they had to tender him. Going into his third or fourth year, the Dolphins decided not to keep him, so he became a free agent.

Turns out while he was playing for the Dolphins, Marlon had a situation arise where he was pulled over by the police, which, by the way, he had failed to tell me. At the time, the NFL had rules about getting pulled over for any reason. I think he pled "no contest." But he didn't understand that pleading no contest meant you were responsible, so he didn't foresee the implications. I think that incident impacted him being released from the Dolphins. By this point, he was married to his high school sweetheart and had one child.

Marlon told me he wanted to play for the San Francisco 49ers. I started calling the personnel guy at the 49ers and said, "Marlon Moore wants to play for the 49ers." I just kept calling and calling and calling. Marlon is from northern California and really wanted to be closer to home, so I was tenacious, which paid off. So after a successful three or four years with the Dolphins, Marlon got a contract with the 49ers. He made the 53-man roster, but then I think about three or four games in, they cut him. Then suddenly all of the Miami Dolphins wide receivers were hurt and they wanted Marlon back.

Marlon had been really upset about how the Dolphins handled things when they released him. He had run into the GM somewhere, and the guy didn't even acknowledge him. Of course, it's really hard to fire people, but bosses need to understand that it hurts athletes when they are let go—it affects their families and injures their egos—being kind in that process is so, so important. Sometimes I think, depending on their personalities, GMs aren't always caring in the way they cut guys, although not all GMs are like that, of course.

When the Dolphins wanted him back, I said, "Marlon, you know you don't have a job right now and they need you."

He went back and played out the season in Miami. This was the time of the scandal regarding Richie Incognito and bullying in the locker room. Marlon was tough and didn't say much about his situation; he was a good locker room guy. At the end of the season, he became a free agent again, and the Cleveland Browns picked him up. The Browns had called and expressed interest in Marlon the year before but he had already committed to the 49ers.

Marlon got a pretty good signing bonus when he signed with the Browns. He played in Cleveland for three years until their GM was released. That same year Marlon was injured and they knew if he made it past the first week they were going to have to pay him for the rest of the season, so they let him go.

Marlon was so upset at this point. He had an ankle injury; he was hurt but felt that he could still play. I knew he shouldn't be playing with his injury. The Browns offered him an injury settlement, which I didn't think he should take, but he needed the money.

For years, I had talked to Marlon about the importance of saving his money. He assured me, "I've saved all my money." What I think happened is when he was in Miami, he got involved with somebody who did not have good intentions. After about three or four games of not getting picked up by a team, he called me. He had a frightened sense of urgency in his voice.

He said, "Jill, I don't have any money."

I said, "What do you mean you don't have any money? You just got a huge injury settlement and you've been playing."

By this time, he had been playing for seven or eight years. He never really told me what happened, but he must have been involved in some kind of deal and lost his money, which was just so sad to me.

What I've learned, and Marlon figured out, is that once players make a minimum salary around a million dollars, those third- or fourth-string guys who are great special teams players will get released so the team can try to find a younger guy who's cheaper. This happens to the last ten or so on the 53-man roster. They don't want to pay those guys that much.

This was a sad time because Marlon had such a great career and deserved better. I always stress to players how vital it is to save all their money for the end of their career.

Marlon did bounce back. He was just recently inducted into the Wall of Fame at his high school. He has a training facility. He and his wife and have two kids and they just bought a new house. Fortunately his wife is also successful in her career.

There's a good side and a bad side about representing a player. Here's what I have found: When players don't make it…let's say they get offered a contract and get into training camp and then they get cut. Sometimes, they can get cut as early as June 1 if they signed a deal at the end of the draft. I always find it interesting that some players never take responsibility for getting cut. Instead, they'll blame the agent who has nothing to do with any of that. Some players think they should get a different agent because they get cut, but really, it's much more prudent to just stick with their agent and be consistent. An agent can be a player's best ally before, during, and after the athlete's career. That's why it's so important to choose the right one!

***

Coming up next is a transparent, vulnerable view into the business of football from a coach's wife's perspective. We've all heard about the commitment and sacrifice it takes to be a coach's wife season after season but we often don't hear about what happens when they're thrown into the trenches of backbiting, lies, bold-face criticism, and complete rejection. How does one recover from that? Or, does one ever recover? How do they pick up the shattered pieces and re-build their life once a one-two punch has been delivered? The following story will answer those questions and more.

Chapter 5

Perspective from a Coach's Wife
Paulette Bonamego

Paulette has been a coach's wife for a long time. Her husband, became the 28th head football coach for his alma mater after a long stint as an NFL Special Teams Coordinator. In this chapter, Paulette tells her story; all of it. I hope as you read on that it will serve as an eye-opening experience and inspire you to keep moving forward no matter what.

I am not a negative person. In fact, I do my very best to try to stay positive, especially in the world we live in. But, if my story can help somebody learn, then it's good to talk about it. We all have a story. We've all been through things that we want to share with others, and we've all been through trials and tribulations that have made us better or smarter. Through my experience I've learned a lot about myself and I've learned a lot about people in general…and I've learned that no one is safe from everything, even if you do everything right.

My husband, and I, are so blessed to be a part of the amazing business of football. We just count our blessings and are grateful that my husband is doing what he loves and I'm enjoying the ride with him.

I've been with my husband now for two decades and we have three amazing kids. We've been a part of several teams in the NFL, and then on a college team, and it's been rewarding because every team has had its benefits and wonderful memories and moments. The best thing to do along the way is learn from what you do, learn from others, move forward, and enjoy the ride.

When my husband became head coach at his alma mater in 2015, it was my goal to be totally involved, supportive, and loving to the players. I had been around football my whole life as my dad was a huge college supporter. Dad graduated from Florida and was an alumni and president of the Gator Club of Jacksonville, where I'm from. I was on the Florida campus as a baby when he and my mom lived in marital housing. I never missed a Florida game my whole life —my dad was a Gator through and through and the university even had scholarships in his name. I was around the players at cookouts at our house and it was just a part of life for me.

When I became a dancer, I performed in half-time shows in the USFL (United States Football League) and the NFL. I ended up taking my dancing abroad and had a ton of fun while learning a lot. Actually, much of what I've learned throughout my life was from my dad and my experience as a professional dancer. I ultimately became a cheerleader in the NFL.

I knew a lot about the challenges of the sports world already so when I met my husband, I already knew the kind of hours coaches kept, I knew about the media, the situations, and the things that can happen. I knew what to do and what not to do. But, alas, no one is 100% safe from situations happening. Things happen because people happen.

In 2015, when he got his first head coaching job, he dove into it. I was so excited and I embraced the players like they were my own. To this day they still call me Mom, and I frequently got texts every from the players because I was such a great part of their lives and they were such a great part of my life for four years. We had three wonderful seasons and the fourth season, unfortunately, didn't go as well, actually, not as we planned at all. It was awful. But that's part of football. You suck it up and get through it. You endure the ups and downs and do your best. Those players were my kids. They're still my kids. I loved every minute of it.

During the fourth season, things changed quickly. New people came in, changes happened rapidly. We wanted to have a good season but we were already somewhat worried about how it would go with all the administrative and leadership changes. We had lost a lot of seniors, and we knew it would be a hard year. We were losing, losing, losing, and things were stressful. People take college games very seriously and wins and losses are all that matter at the end of the day. We knew we had to suck it up and get through the season, but things just kept going south. We muddled through, did the best we could, and tried to keep the players' chins up. The only thing you can do is go to work every day and do the best you can do with the situation you have—and that's what we did. No regrets…well, maybe a couple on my end for letting my heart get the best of me.

Okay, so during the season, coaches' wives and kids are in the stands watching the game with everybody else. We hear when those around us say mean things about our children or husband or a bad play call, or about one of the players. Fans don't realize who might be sitting around them and when they mouth off negativity, it's very hurtful to coaches' wives, and especially the kids who are hearing bad things said about their dads. You have to have thick skin to survive.

Let me say this: coaches' kids are amazing and I give them mega credit because they go through so much and it's not their choice; it's Dad's choice and Mom's choice, and the kids just know that this is what Dad does and the negative comments are simply part of the package deal. Coaches' kids are taught to ignore it, look away, not read anything. Sometimes, the cruelty is in your face or literally behind your back when you're sitting in your seat so it's very hard to ignore. People are intentionally and freely making comments about what play sucked, or who on the team sucks, or they're shouting out to fire the defense coordinator, fire the coach, fire everybody, sometimes knowing full well that the wives and kids are sitting in front of them. For some odd reason they think the wife will go back and tell her husband and he'll listen and make it all better. They feel good for venting, knowing you heard it. That's just how it is. That's the bad side of it. That's the negative side. I've heard it all. At this point, there's nothing anyone can say that surprises me. I've had people say things to my face, I've had things said behind my back, my kids have had things said to them at school.

My oldest son had to deal with this stuff. One day a couple of kids from high school were waiting at the bus stop, wanting to know where Coach's son was because they wanted to beat him up for some nonsense about certain players having a bad game the night before, or something like that. We've been through some crazy stuff. I'm giving you a glimpse into the bad part of the sport because a coach gets paid to coach yet he has to take a lot of crap too.

When he was head coach, we had lost a difficult conference game by one point in the final moment. We probably had four or five games that season that we should have won and we didn't, but it's a game of inches and we weren't having any luck at all that last season, especially in this game.

During the game, I had been entertaining a bunch of people in the hospitality suite and after the game was over, there was popcorn everywhere. I was on my hands and knees picking up popcorn and trying to clean my suite because I didn't want the cleaning people to see the mess; it was a habit of mine, I always cleaned it before the cleaners came. They would always laugh, "Ms. Bonamego you don't have to clean up, that's why we're here." But that's how I am so that's what I was doing.

I had cleaned up the suite, and I was rushing to get home to get my daughter ready for her homecoming dance—it was her first one, and I needed to do her hair and get her to the school and we were behind schedule because the game had gotten out in the evening and we were supposed to have already been at the school for the dance.

As I was leaving the suite, I had a tray of food in one hand and a flower arrangement in the other, and that was when the confrontation with the media person happened as he approached me with some extremely hurtful words and name calling—I remember feeling very offended as I've never been called a name like that before by a man—I was hurt and shocked and instead of walking away, I decided to go right back. There was some yelling; it was just adults being stupid and having a disagreement, and it should have just ended with that. But my concern at that moment was to get out of there and get home to my daughter. We also had a recruiting dinner immediately afterward so I had to get myself together and get over to the restaurant to meet a couple of our players who were hosting the dinner—we had a full agenda after the game. I had played hostess to about 20 people, plus others who were coming and going—to watch the game, drink, and socialize throughout the four hours. I'm serving and trying to enjoy the experience. We were winning most of the time so it was a decent game, but I didn't have time for any arguing that afternoon, that's for sure. But, you just never know what's going to happen in this profession.

As a coach's wife, especially the head coach's wife, I'm certainly not obligated to protect anybody. The players are big boys, they can protect themselves. But as a mom and as a wife and as a woman, part of our intuition and our motherly instinct is to stick up for our kids, or at least defend them to some degree. I've always walked away because I know to walk away. But this day I didn't. You can't predict your boiling point, and you can never let your guard down.

I didn't say anything hurtful; I didn't cuss, I just said my piece about the kids and how hard they worked, how great they were, and about how we need to lift them up. I gave this media person a little one-minute spiel about how incredible these kids are off the field and for him to beat them down when they were already down was unfathomable.

Allow me to interject a thought here: when you're having a bad season, a lot of times there can be dead air space and commentators, play callers, people in the media, need to use that dead space to talk about how amazing the kids are, what they do in the off-season, how many missionary trips they go on, how many instruments they play, what they're planning on doing after college, or what they want to do with their lives after they're done playing in the pros, or just about what they do for society, for people, for their town. There are so many topics that can shed positive light on a team when they're not doing well instead of beating them down or talking about how bad they look. In my defense and in that situation I was only stating how great these kids are—my point to the man was that there are other routes to take other than blasting them when they're already down. I was held accountable for my actions yet all I was doing was taking a minute to defend these kids. But hey, you can't do that. You have to walk away.

I very rarely had a drink in my suite and particularly that day there was just no time. At away games if I tailgated with the families I would join in and we would toast and have some innocent and harmless fun, but that's different—I'm not hosting people. But when we're home in our territory and I've got important people, or family and people I care about, I try to enjoy the moment, win or lose. That day I had so many kids in my suite; I remember holding babies and feeding them cupcakes and cookies and just having a good time.

I always had a full stock of drinks because there were so many people who came to enjoy the suite; alumni, people from the school, and I was always very welcoming to everybody. I would let anybody in there and it got to the point where after several years nobody would ask; they'd just show up. That's why I always made sure I had what I knew everyone liked. And that particular day with the homecoming dance, there were some special guests in the suite. My mindset was focused on serving and making sure everyone was having a good time, not on drinking. That day was about winning the game and helping my daughter get ready for her first dance in high school. It was a big deal. Even after the loss, as bad as my heart was hurting, I was excited about getting home to her and having a positive ending to the day.

After the confrontation with the media person, the rest just spiraled from there, without me even knowing. Immediately following the confrontation, I experienced my first ever panic attack.

Nobody had ever challenged me like that before, especially the name calling, yet I knew that somehow I had to keep it together and try to put my game face on for my kids. I didn't want them to know that their mom was completely broken.

My husband and I have been through all the coaches' stuff you can possibly go through; been fired, hired, playoff games and Super Bowl runs, big wins and big losses but that incident was the first time in my husband's career that we've been trashed in the media. It's the first time in my husband's career that I, as a coach's wife, literally could not breathe, I couldn't think coherently. Looking back now through all the weeks and months that have passed, I know that I emotionally broke down because of all the stress from that confrontation. I had set my expectations so high for my husband and I really did try hard to do all the right things and love everybody and support everybody. I had always had a positive mentality and this is the one time that I literally knew I was broken. I wanted to crawl in a hole. The next day, in my ignorance and naivety, I expected a phone call with an apology.

After the first season, I learned not to tune in to any media. I don't read the paper, I don't read any commentary, I don't listen to any of the radio stuff. It's not because I don't like some of the commentators, we have a lot of friends in the business who do a great job. From the first year on, I couldn't handle the negativity—as a head coach's wife I couldn't believe I was listening to so much negative talk about kids. Because I had been with my husband around the college circuit, I was blind and deaf to what people felt comfortable spewing. I didn't expect the negative tone when people would talk about 18- to 20-year-old kids who are playing their hearts out. That's why I always kept the volume off. People would ask me if I had heard this person, or that person? I would always respond,

"Nope, don't want to know, please don't tell me. It's not my concern."

This one media person who confronted me after the game had an extremely condescending, sarcastic, mean-spirited mentality. That kind of attack is a lose-lose for all involved—no one is going to benefit from being ugly or being ugly back or trying to defend. In retrospect, I should have known to just to walk away...I do know. But I was by myself, I had no one there with me. When you're cornered by another person, especially if it's the opposite sex, a male on female situation, it's very intimidating. As a woman I think my first instinct was to protect myself; it was like a big dog backing a little puppy into the corner. The little dog is going to try to defend itself even if it shouldn't, and I think in my situation, I felt like I needed to defend myself.

I should have never been in that situation to begin with, because I always questioned why I was alone in that area. Even though it's a private floor on the press level, people can get up there, and they did. Fans got up there all the time without passes. The first and second year I asked for cameras outside of my suite because I always felt a little uneasy at times when complete strangers would pop in and just kind of hang around or stare down or make little comments; it's not the safest feeling when you feel like you're being invaded in a space that should be exclusively yours. If only we had cameras, the story would have had a different ending. If only.

The confrontation lasted less than a couple of minutes, and, like I said, we were just going back and forth, being stupid. I felt like I was disrespected and I was obviously physically shaken. I kept telling myself I'm stronger than that, I've been through worse, I've been through bad things before. But everybody has a breaking point, and you just hope that it doesn't happen on your husband's time. If I was to break down, I'd rather it be at home.

The stadium security staff that night were no help whatsoever; they just sat around with their hands in their pockets, and I think it was a freak show for them to watch the head coach's wife have a meltdown. As for me, I just wanted help getting out of there. I begged for help, I was so totally in a state of panic and shock—my whole thought process was off kilter—I just wanted to get to my husband and my daughter. My daughter had been calling my phone during this time but I was unable to pick up. I asked the security people several times for help getting out of the stadium but they just kind of stood there like what do you want us to do?

So, as I said, the next day after I woke up, I was thinking they're going to apologize, they're going to call and make this right.

My husband was fired at the end of the season, literally two minutes after the last game was over. Phone call. Boom. Done. I realize now that I was just a pawn in the game. The thing is: the university never mentioned anything about the media person incident until the day after he was fired, then all of a sudden the headline was splattered all over the front page: Paulette Bonamego was banned from the stadium due to a confrontation with a play-by-play announcer. The article stated, "It's unclear how much she had to drink." Well, I didn't have anything to drink! When you find out about a newspaper headline that says the head coach's wife gets banned from the stadium, it is humiliating beyond words. Emotionally, I still can't read the article...probably never will.

The university's solution was to keep me and this other person apart...by banning ME. I knew it couldn't have been because anyone was scared of me because I'm harmless. I've never been in a fight in my life, but this whole situation turned completely opposite, and because I'm not an employee of the school and the media person was a part-time employee or part of the union, or whatever, he's protected and I'm not, so I have to go. And that was my breaking point.

That's when I realized this was as low as it could get for me in this business. My personality and mindset involve always being supportive of everybody, and acting respectful toward everybody and just trying to fit in. The funny thing is that anyone who knows me knows that I've always been one for doing the right thing. I don't think I've ever even gotten a speeding ticket in my life and to have this happen just devastated me. When you're in this business you donate your time, your money, your family; you sacrifice so much. And it's not like you expect a certain outcome from doing all that, but when the opposite happens, it really does mess with your psyche.

The university did what they called an investigation, and that meant if they talked to one person they could say they did an investigation because the word itself is kind of a broad term. No one in my suite that day was ever talked to. Nobody was ever called in or questioned about whether or not they saw me drinking, but they would have had to say, "No, of course not; Paulette was being the normal head coach's wife doing the normal thing." The "investigation" consisted of talking to the people who were there after the verbal argument, because no one was there when it happened except me and the media person.

I never in my life thought this type of thing would happen to a head coach's wife, or to any coach's wife. In hindsight, I think it was all part of a very well-orchestrated way to get rid of us. And the fact of the matter is that my husband loves me to death, and I love him to death and the best way to get to somebody sometimes is through the person they love.

My eyes are wide open now.

The odd thing is that I got banned from the whole campus because I defended the kids on the team in a brief one-minute conversation. I was told I couldn't step foot on the campus for any reason. I can laugh a little bit about it now, but it's taken me several months to feel okay. Not great, just okay. I have a long way to go. My heart is still broken, my emotions and my mental state over what happened is not okay yet; it was just so traumatizing. When this incident happened, we still had a whole season to get through. Now, I wasn't allowed to go and have lunch with my husband. I wasn't allowed to go to the recruiting dinners. I wasn't allowed to go to anything associated with football. I wasn't allowed to call or receive calls or texts from the players nor the parents. I couldn't meet anyone for lunch…nothing. I couldn't even take my kids to their activities on campus. I had to pull them from everything. I couldn't talk about the situation in detail. I was basically told I couldn't do anything on or related to that campus.

For several months I lived in a very secluded situation where I was scared to go anywhere because I was afraid I'd run into a player or a professor because I wasn't allowed to even talk to anybody who was affiliated with the school in any capacity; I was bullied into being scared to death. I lived that way for months, and so did my husband; he was trying to coach and at the same time wonder how his wife was doing at home; his wife who was completely shut down and closed off from everybody.

The underlying, unspoken message behind it all was that if I stepped on campus they were going to fire my husband, which, obviously, they did anyway. If I violated the ban, it would be grounds for his dismissal.

I think the hardest part for me was not being able to text the players or call them back if they called me. Because you have to remember, I was like the team mom, and for many of these kids I was used to talking to them daily. Several of them would text me things out of the blue, whether it was a girlfriend issue or question or asking for advice. Some of the kids' moms would call me and say, "Hey, I haven't seen [son's name] for the day and they're not calling me back, is everything okay?" I would text them right back and say oh he's doing great, they're just in the middle of these exams or it's a hard week or I'll talk to him and make sure he gets back to you right away. And then I'd call the player and say, "Hey, call your mom!" It was a daily thing for me to be involved with the players. I was always at practice because I wanted to watch them from the bleachers. They loved me being around and I loved being there—and that was all taken away.

So when all of a sudden I couldn't respond to texts I think a lot of the kids thought that I had bailed on them because we were losing. Like, wow we're losing and she disappears. Hmm. That was really hard for me because I would never walk away from a team or players just because we're losing. Emotionally, the whole situation and all the ramifications took their toll on me. I couldn't even watch the games on TV without crying. I think I cried every day, all day, for months. When my kids came home from school, I would put on my game face for them and that was extremely difficult because I was dying inside.

I was wrong in that I should not have gone right back to respond to the media person. I should have walked away just like I've done for 20 years. But when you have a panic attack, you can't breathe, you're scared, you can't focus, your thoughts come out as rants, and everything is discombobulated. My knees were weak. I had a bum leg

79

anyway from knee surgery, so I was not in the best position physically but I couldn't get myself out of there fast enough. I didn't know at the time that I was having a full-fledged panic attack because I had never had one before yet I knew something wasn't right with me. I felt really sick. I had to run to the bathroom because I thought I was going to get sick right there in the hallway.

Don't get me wrong, I'm a strong person. I've been an advocate and fundraiser for women who have been sexually abused and survivors of rape and I used my platform as a coach's wife to talk to young women about my story so I'm no rookie to talking to people. I've been through things myself. But I'm a survivor, a fighter and I'm not going to sit back and just let someone walk all over me if they're verbally hurting me.

My freedom of speech was muffled by the university, but not only that, the night of the incident, my panic attack was misinterpreted for drinking. So basically I was punished for having a panic attack and that's extremely offensive to me.

My kids had to go to school and hear other kids say, "So your mom is fighting and drinking at the games?" They would come home crying because of the stuff that was being said which was all lies and inconsistencies. In small towns and college towns, it can be hard on the kids—you just do the best you can to keep your own kids safe and you try to remember these are just people with opinions and some of these people don't know what they're talking about. Most people don't know the inside stuff, they simply make assumptions based on what they've heard.

So my husband had been fired and I haven't been to the campus for seven weeks. I've been at home in a cocoon, behaving myself like a child in the corner on a timeout and all the while just scared to death. I vegetated in my house, very depressed, and pretty much shutting everybody off, including my own family back home because I didn't want them to worry. My family had caught wind of the incident and were very concerned, especially my parents. My uncle, the preacher, was flabbergasted because he knew my behavior that night did not resemble who I really am as a person, a woman. My family knew that something bad had to happen that night for me to even get into the argument because I'm so passive, I get along with everybody. It's sad, but now I know how vulnerable we really are in this business.

Time heals but you never forget. My kids have been dramatically affected and right now I'm focusing on getting them to embrace a more positive outlook about this business. They love football. They love what their dad does. But they're very hesitant now to talk to other kids about what their dad does, and when people bring it up, they avoid the topic altogether.

The university was getting flak about letting my husband go but in the end their little scheme worked. We were gone.

I saved a text that my husband had sent me earlier on the same day he was fired; it was the most heart-warming amazing text from him about his job as head coach and how much he's loved every minute. He texted, we're going to handle this with pride and dignity and we're going to just walk away and appreciate and enjoy the good that came from this and hold our heads up high. He said I love you and included a couple of Bible verses. He sent that text to me two seconds before he got the phone call that he was fired. For him to text me we're going to get through this, knowing I'd been through hell and back for weeks and weeks and weeks, was very significant.

And then the very next day I'm front page news for a one-minute argument that happened eight weeks prior. I now had a 20-year-old college kid writing in his school newspaper about me; lying about me in order to damage me for the almighty dollar, and there's nothing I can do about it. The fact that people can go so low to come after a woman, after a wife, for their own gain—just to make money.

If I can help at least one other person learn from my story, I'll be happy knowing someone else avoided an emotional wrecking ball situation. The only thing I did wrong was I didn't walk away after the media person called me horrible names. Was there an argument? Yes, but that was the extent of it. Yet embellishing what happened makes for a better story, and a better, juicier story is what people want. Unfortunately, that's how it can be in this business.

***

Here are some take-away lessons that might help you if you're a coach's wife reading this.

First, if you are a coach's wife in any situation where you are getting questioned by anybody at a school, that's when you say, "You know what, I need to talk to my agent or attorney." Tell whoever is questioning you to ask their questions in writing and that you will respond in writing.

The school, the team, wherever you're at, whatever you're doing, they're always going to have their best interests first. Not yours. Their job is to protect the integrity of the school. And that's fine. It should be that way. They should protect the institution and the students and the people there. But you have to remember that you have rights as well and you need to exercise them. A lot of contracts might say that you have to participate in any investigation that's going on at the university, and that's fine. But it doesn't say you have to go in front of people and spill your guts.

Second, I wish I would have gone in with representation. I needed someone to tell me, don't sit down with anybody because they're there to protect the school, don't go in there and offer any information unless you have a set of questions.

Third, manage your expectations as a coach's wife, especially a head coach's wife. There are a lot of responsibilities that, even though you're not being paid, people expect from you; the team, your husband, society, the school, fans, the town. You feel a certain sense of responsibility for the staff. You worry about the other coaches' wives and their kids and then when your husband gets fired as head coach, it affects everybody on the staff. A new coach comes up and they may get rid of everybody, or they may keep half, and it's all out of your control. If you manage your expectations, it helps you not to be so disappointed when things don't go well at any level.

At this point, my husband and I are trying to go about our business and be appreciative for the time we had there. Life will go on and we will recover.

Segment II

The X's and O's of Sports Representation

Chapter 6

Welcome to the X's & O's of Sports Representation!

This section takes an in-depth look into the sports agent industry. What I'm going to share with you comes from my years of experience and industry knowledge and will provide you with an up close and personal view into what it takes to become an NFL sports agent.

The material I'm presenting here serves two audiences: 1) it's for those who are starting out and want to know how to run a NFL sports agent business, and 2) it's for those who are already in the business and want to do a better job than they are currently doing. What you will learn from this section is the step-by-step process of exactly how to run a sports agent business and the process I personally use. I think my process is unique as it differs from the status quo of other sports agents. I have a 25-page workbook that I go through with my clients, and I also have a different fee structure than most agents. If you follow the process I lay out for you, you, too, will be a successful representative for players. I've been a sports agent for 30 years and you can do the same. Let's dive in!

Step 1: Business Fundamentals: Education & Licensing

The first thing you need to be an NFL sports agent, is you have to be qualified and you do need a certain educational background. You need an undergraduate degree and you most definitely need a master's degree to be certified with the NFL Players Association. I highly recommend that you go to law school. If you haven't done all of that, then you may not be ready for the rest of the material in this section.

Here's what I have: I have an undergraduate degree and I have a juris doctorate. You might say, well, okay, I have that so now what? You have to be certified with the NFL Players Association. By the way, you can't just call up and get certified. It takes about a year. You have to go through a course, learn the CBA (collective bargaining agreement) take an exam, and pass the exam, pass a background check, pay your fee, and get insurance. Expect this process to take about a year out of your life. If you think you can just wake up one day and decide to be a sports agent, it doesn't work that way in the current model.

If you want to be an agent for another sport, say the MLB, check with their union to see what the requirements are. I do know in major league baseball you have to sign a player first and then you can get certified. For the NBA or boxing or any other sport, again, you must check with their unions first to find out about their requirements.

The bottom line is that anybody who wants to be an agent should have a law degree, because you're negotiating contracts and with NFL clients, you're interpreting a very complex CBA.

Check all the state laws because you have to be a registered sports agent in the states where you are recruiting players. By the way, you have to do that BEFORE you start talking to players, not after. I am registered in California, Arizona, Utah, Oregon, Colorado, and North Carolina and New Mexico. (West Coast) There are a lot of players in Texas and Florida so you may want to get registered there as well. Typically, I'm going to look at about a hundred players, and from that hundred I'll see what state that player I'm recruiting lives in and if I like who he is and have a good connection with him, and feel like I have a good chance, then I would get registered in that state as well.

If you're an attorney in multiple states, make sure you keep one of your licenses active although you don't have to be a licensed attorney. I like to keep at least one of my licenses active; as of this writing my Utah and Maryland licenses are active.

After you register in each of the states you want to recruit in, it's a requirement that you register with each compliance department at each university. Do your homework and find out what the rules are. For instance, I do a lot of recruiting at UCLA, ASU, U of A, University of Utah, Stanford, Cal, Colorado, and Fresno State, basically the Pac 12 (Mountain West). Doesn't matter if it's a big school or a small school,

Before you I recruit I register with their compliance department and I get to know their compliance department. Not only that, but once you do sign a player from that particular school, you should send a letter to the compliance department letting them know that you've signed a player there. I did not know this rule until recently when I was informed that it was a required state law in Missouri. The compliance officer told me, "Yeah you're also supposed to send a letter to the compliance department." That was the first time I had heard that rule. Not every single school has that rule, but I think it's a good rule to practice. After notifying the compliance department, it would be an excellent idea to also notify the head coach and let him know that you're representing this player and tell him, "We'd love to have your support in talking with this player to the pro teams."

After you get registered, after you get certified, and you've talked to all the schools, and the coaches, then you're finally ready to figure out what the rules are at each specific school to find out when you can start contacting the players.

Step 2: Business Fundamentals/Developing Your Brand

Now it's time to create your brand and I can't overstate the importance of building a strong brand. Before you start a sports agent business it's imperative that you ask yourself, "Who am I? What do I represent? Why do I do what I do?" Go to YouTube and watch a powerful video by Simon Sinek where he talks about your Why. He also wrote a book on the topic called Start with Why which will revolutionize the way you do business.

When I asked that same question of Why, that's how I created my brand. After examining everything I had done for 30 years, I discovered I was all about protection, advocacy and trust and that's exactly what I want to do for my clients. I want to protect them, I want to be an advocate for them, and I want to be their trusted advisor. For my website I picked an Irish logo and if you look inside the logo there are three footballs. I'm Irish and I was married on St. Patrick's Day; this represents family, and I really consider my clients as my family and I treat them like family.

Because I'm clear on my Why, when I first meet with a client, the first thing I tell them is that I'm about protection, advocacy, and trust. I say, "If those are important values to you then we will align and this will work out." So what I'm trying to say to you, from the very beginning is that you have to decide who you are, what you represent and decide on three or four words you'll put in your logo.

At this point, you may be asking, "How am I going to create a logo? I don't know anything about graphic design." Well, there's a freelance platform called Fiverr. You can hire somebody on Fiverr to create a logo for you unless you happen to know someone who will do it for you as a favor, or you can pay to have it done. But for Fiverr, you describe what you want based on who you are and what you represent, the Seller will provide some samples and you'll have a logo for less than 20 bucks most of the time.

Next you must ask yourself is, "What is my core purpose?" I determined that my core purpose was protection for individuals and families contractually for financial and physical well-being in a volatile, stressful environment. My core purpose is why I get up every day, and it drives what I tell my clients. You have to decide on your own core purpose. It's important that you talk to your client about your values and core purpose, because if you attract people who have different values than you from the beginning, I can guarantee you, it is not going to work out. Aligning your values and core purpose with your potential clients is really important because you're going to invest a lot of time in this client—you need to be talking about your core message and your core purpose.

My core message says Informed representation and unconditional support with the intended outcome of preparation, promotion, protection, advocacy and trust in a volatile environment. My core message expresses my core values: I'm about protection, advocacy and trust. I have a logo, I have a core purpose, and I have a core message. When I meet with a client, the first thing I talk about is the significance of my logo, my core purpose, and my core message. So before you even think about getting clients, you need to spend the time laying the framework. Take the time now so you don't waste a lot of time with clients who do not support your core message and your core values.

Next create a constitution which is basically affirmative statements. For instance, I do anything to protect my clients. Everyone who works for me is going to be trustworthy. Everyone who works for me is going to put the clients first. My affirmation statements form my constitution and that's how I'm going to run my business.

Recap: 1) create a brand, 2) create a core purpose, 3) write a core message, and 4) create a constitution.

Step 3: Business Fundamentals/An Agent's Average Earnings

Show me the money! You have probably seen the movie Jerry Maguire where one of the clients says, "Show me the money." I have to admit, talking about money is my favorite topic—and it's the one topic you should pay the closest attention to. Why? Because, if you don't think about the money from the beginning, you will be out of business quick.

When I first meet with a player I tell them the actual dollar amount they're going to pay me to represent them. It's important to be up front and honest when you're talking dollars. How much are you going to make as an agent from the player?

Your compensation depends on whether your client is a first-round pick, a fourth-round pick, or a seventh-round pick, and what you decide to charge. Could be 3%, 2% or 1%, but whatever it is, this is the amount you, the agent, will get paid only if the player makes the 53-man roster.

Now, if you have a first-round pick, you could charge them 1% because your fee over a three-year period would be $174,000. Divide that amount by three and you'll come up with a number of what you get each year. If you have a fourth-round pick and this person makes the 53-man roster for three years, the following is what you would make: $70,000 at 3%, $46,000 at 2%, and $23,000 at 1%. That's if they make it for three years.

Now, a seventh-round will pay you, if you're charging 3% AND they make the 53-man roster, and I say if, and that's because it's a very hard thing to do, and I'm going to talk about that problem in a minute. The seventh-round pick is going to pay you an average of $53,000 at 3%, $35,000 at 2%, and $17,000 at 1%.

Why do I tell the players this first? Because I have found, over 30 years of doing this, the one thing players don't like to do is write the check to their agent. By the time they write the check to their agent, they've already gone through the draft, training camp, and then you finally bill them at the end of September. If they make the 53-man roster and they've made it for four games, you're only going to charge them for the first four games. If they've gotten a large signing bonus you've probably charged them for that percentage as well.

I talk to them about these numbers from the beginning, because it is a huge problem when you meet with a player and they tell you, "I want you to give me $50,000 to sign with you." No! Don't do that. For one thing, it's an inducement, it's against the rules, and that's not at all what you should do. I can pretty much guarantee you that you will lose money if you go that route. There are only 32 guys every year who are going to be in the first round. Since you are just starting out as an agent, it is unlikely you're going to get a first-round pick. And if you get lucky and do get a first-round pick, of course you can then charge them 3%, 2% or 1% to be adequately compensated for your time.

For the record, I don't think anybody should train anywhere but their school, if your client is drafted in the fourth round, and you give them $20,000 for training. You're going to lose money in your first year because that's what the client will owe you if your fee is 3% of their salary. If you're a seventh-round pick you're going to lose money for sure. If you charge them 3%, you're going to get $17,000 which is minimum salary, but 3% of that and you will have already lost money in the first year. This is why I am adamantly opposed to ever, ever, ever giving a player money for any reason. The minute you do that you will become a bank. They will treat you like a bank, and you will never get past that.

Step 4: Business Fundamentals/"Profit First": Navigating Expenses & Building Your Business

In this section, let's go back to the "show me the money" concept. There are quite a few expenses that you're going to incur as a sports agent. Before you read another line, I suggest you go on Amazon and buy a book called Profit First. This intensely practical book by Mike Michalowicz describes how you should be paying yourself as you go, putting away 2% or 3% to profit or as Mike says, 30% to "owner's compensation." After that, you put aside 15% for taxes and then you see how much money you have left. The Profit First concept teaches you that if you can't put away "profit money" for yourself, and you don't have any owner's compensation, and you can't afford to pay your taxes, you essentially don't have a business. The bottom line is you need to learn about money and finances.

The following are some activities that are going to cost you a lot of money as an agent that have nothing to do with any particular client.

1. Travel. One event that you must go to every year is the Combine that's where the annual meeting with the NFL Players Association is held and that's where they tell the NFL Agents all the newest information. The entire NFL is there so you have time to network with everybody. You'll also be attending a lot of sports networking events so you can connect yourself with others in the industry.

2. Acquiring a client. You need to put a cap on how much you're willing to spend on acquiring a client. If you're traveling all over the place meeting with a hundred different players, that can get really, really costly. Toward the end of the process, I meet with most of the players one on one but before that I get it narrowed down to ten to 20 guys that I know I have a chance of actually getting. It comes down to the potential client deciding that they're going to pick me, or maybe they have it down to three agents and I'm in the running.

3. You must have a website. A place where you can send potential clients and their families to find out more about you. The important thing to remember is to build a website or have one built for you that's user-friendly and one that Google gets along with—WordPress and Google are best friends. Ideally, you need a website that lets you manage the backend on your own without having to pay someone monthly to do it for you.

You need to use a variety of marketing tools to market your clients, you are going to be flying a lot of different places, you need to make a lot of connections and you need to go to a lot of networking events so you can get to know the people in the sports industry. All this can be very expensive. Create a budget on how much you're going to spend every year because if you don't watch it, travel expenses can quickly spiral out of control.

Step 5: Signing Clients: Identifying Prospects

Let's talk more about identifying talent. The odds of making it in the NFL is really not that great. I actually consider the odds to be a really bad math problem. In fact, the average year, every year, 327 players are invited to the Combine. The 327 players are "allegedly" the best 327 players in the country. You have to identify and sign at least one of these 327. From the guys who got invited to the Combine, 19 of them never signed a contract, 90 were not drafted but signed a free-agent contract, 218 got drafted, 37 got drafted and never attended the Combine. The whole game is identifying the 327 players that are getting invited to the Combine.

I get at least ten emails a day from players who are simply not good enough. I don't want to represent those guys. They need to be invited to the Combine, then you know that they at least have a chance of getting drafted and making a team.

So, now I can hear you asking, "How do I identify talent?" I'll tell you how. You need to learn how to look at film and identify who's good and who's not. If you don't know how to do that, you probably shouldn't get in the NFL agent game. I can go to a practice and watch a player's feet; take an offensive lineman for example. I can watch him and see whether he's got good feet, is he the right size, does he have production, has he sustained a minimum of injuries. After observing all that, I'll conclude, okay, this guy looks like he's got potential. What do I do next? I'll call one of my scouting friends and ask, "Who do you have on your list with a draftable grade from, let's say Arizona State University?" And he'll tell me "Well, I've got this guy and this guy," and if he doesn't bring up the person's name I'm talking about, I'll bring up his name. The scout might reply back, "Yeah, I think he's good but you might want to check with some other scouts because I wasn't in charge of that particular player group, or I didn't look at three games, I only looked at one." That means I may have to do a little more research.

Who else can I talk to? The head coach of that player's team. The head coach is going to be able to tell me, "Well, a few scouts have come through, this guy you're asking about has been very productive, he's a good kid, he hasn't had very many injuries, he's a super hard worker and he's a good person."

Who else is on my list to talk to? Their position coach. I would say, "Tell me about this player. How is he to work with? Is he consistent? Is he coachable? Is he a good kid? Is he a great player? How many scouts have called you about this player?"

Another person to discuss players with is the strength coach. The strength coach is going to tell you whether the player finishes his work or not. This is really important because in the weight room when a player doesn't push as hard as they should, they're going to have a tough time in the end really succeeding in the NFL.

Additional people to talk to would be student managers and people who work in the office, who can tell you how your prospect treats other people. They might not be able to identify talent, but they can identify character.

Another person to talk to is the Sports Information Director who works closely with high-profile clients. They can tell you how your prospect reacts and relates to the media.

The bottom line: before you start, you have to learn how to identify talent. Pull up some YouTube videos and start watching film on players. See if you can identify why one player is better than another, depending on position, and keep in mind that each position is different. Each team might even have a job description for a particular position. For example; a team might have a specific job description for a punter. The team may want a lefty punter who has played in cold weather, who can directional punt really well, has good hang time and distance as well as consistency. If the potential punter is right-footed and hasn't played in cold weather, the team is probably not going to pick them. The team probably wants the punter to be a certain height, preferably taller, six feet three inches at a minimum. What I've described is a possible job description for a punter. A coach in a warm weather climate may want another type of punter so you have to figure out what the job descriptions are for each position and make sure the guy fits the description on top of him being a great player.

Step 6: Signing Clients/Recruiting Clients

Once you know how to identify talent, now it's time to decide from a numbers perspective how many players to start with and how many to whittle your list down to. I'll start by giving you a harsh-reality stat. Every year 775 NEW players are going to be signed in the NFL. Most of those are going to be signed right after the draft as undrafted free agents. But do you know how many of those guys are going to even make the team? Only 176. So again, the numbers game is not very great. Why is it so low? Because most teams are maybe going to turn over five guys on their roster and the new player has to beat out a player who previously made the 53-man roster. It's not very easy—you basically have to take another man's job.

Here's the way I approach the numbers game: First, I come up with 100 players each year after evaluating the talent and doing a little bit of research. I then start to contact those players on social media. Sometimes I DM (direct message) them, and that's after I've checked with the compliance department to make sure that I'm following the compliance rule at the school and the state. It's really important that you follow the rules and believe me they're different everywhere. After I find out what the rules are I get in touch directly with the player typically on Twitter, Instagram, or Snapchat. However, the ultimate goal is to get their cell number and email address so you can communicate with them frequently.

You can start out with an introduction similar to hey, these are my values, I've been watching you, I think you're a great player. Start to get to know the player, start building a relationship with the player. Once you've built a relationship with the player, you're going to need to watch their college games on TV, and probably attend some of their games.

What I ultimately try to do is get a meeting with that player, in December preferably, at the end of their senior year. Why do I wait that long? Because honestly, I've met with players early, I've met with them in between, and I've met with them at the end, and I've found there's a huge difference in the timing. My goal throughout the process is to build a relationship with them in some way. Sometimes the best way to do that is to have people who are close to them recommend you.

If you're a new agent it's going to be hard for you to get a recommendation because you don't have any players you are currently representing. If you have represented players from that school they will recommend you, but there might be other people who you already have established relationships with who can refer you; like coaches. In my case, since I'm a coach's kid and a coach's wife, (I realize my situation is unique and helpful) I know a lot of coaches, so I might call a coach and ask who is influencing the specific player I'm interested in. Find out who's influencing him and try to get in touch with those people.

By the end of my identifying and recruiting process, I'll get my list down to about 20 players who are interested in me, and 20 players who I'm interested in, and then I will do everything I can to find out who the decision-makers are for each player and set a time to meet with them in person. I suggest doing this usually in December, after they're done playing. It may be late into January if they are in one of the later bowl games.

Step 7: Signing Clients/Signing an SRA

Once I get a client, every single client signs what is called a Standard Representation Agreement which is a contract created by the NFL Players Association. Within the document there are a few important boxes to check. For instance, there's a Disclosure form. What does that mean? If you represent other individuals in the NFL, for example, coaches, like I do, you have to check the box that says yes, I do represent coaches in the NFL and personnel, and then you'd have to have a separate sheet to fill out that lists all the coaches and/or AD's (Athletic Directors) or anybody else that you represent in case there is a potential conflict of interest. The fact that you represent others within the NFL simply has to be disclosed to the player.

Another box to check is whether or not you've entered into any other agreements with the player. I've told you to not do that; don't do training agreements, don't do housing agreements. None of those. But if you do, you'd better make sure you check the box that says you have a different agreement about training. Typically, the agreements protect the agent. To protect yourself, the separate agreement should say that if that player decides to leave they have to pay you back and/or they have to pay you back once they get a signing bonus, or they have to pay you back under all circumstances. Let's say they borrowed money from you for training—I would never just give that to them, they need to pay the money back as it can't be an expense of yours. It's too much money as I talked about before.

It's imperative that you complete the SRA correctly or it will get kicked back and you'll have to start over. Thankfully, it's online although you will need a wet signature. Your client has to print it out, sign it, and scan it back to you. Then you have to print it out, sign it, scan it, and send it back to the NFLPA. You can't do an e-sign on the SRA. This is a legal document and they want to make sure the signatures are the actual signatures of the player and the agent.

I can't stress enough the need to carefully review all the boxes on the form when you're filling it out and it's at this point that you need to decide what you're going to charge. I am of the opinion that if you're not paying for training and you don't have a bunch of expenses, you can charge a lower percentage, or you can charge a flat fee, or you can charge on a sliding scale if you want. I have done all three. You should charge at least the minimum 1% or 2%, because they always need help; meaning you don't know when they're going to need help. You don't know when they're going to get cut. So they need somebody there for them—they might need you to market them to a new team if they do get cut.

I will do a sliding scale or a flat fee for players who have been in the league for a long time—maybe they just need someone to renegotiate because they don't like their current agent.

You've got to decide what works for you and what pencils for you but really if you don't give a player any money you can charge a very fair fee.

If your client is a first-round pick, that's a whole different ball game. With a first-round pick, it's going to pencil even if you provide some money for training although I'll say it again, I am adamantly opposed to doing that because I don't think that's the best choice.

Step 8: Prepping Players/Goal-Setting & Scheduling

Okay, congratulations, you've got your first client. Now what do you do? I send them a planner. I have a specific planner that I order and send to my clients. Why? Because I want to get on the same page with them for the whole next year. (academicgameplan.com professional planner)

Once I send the planner to my client, I set a phone appointment which I record. I do this over Skype. Why do I record it? Because I don't want them to forget what they said. I will share the audio recording with them so they have a copy as well.

During that recorded conversation, I'm going to talk about the importance of creating a strong brand, I will ask them to tell me about who they are and what they represent, and they need to tell me what their long-term goals are, what their short-term goals are, and what they want to do after football is over. This is where I set the ten-year plan, the five-year plan, the one-year plan, and the six-month plan.

A lot of players focus on the first six months because they're obsessed about their training schedule, yet that is just such a small part of their representation.

During the call, you will review the NFL schedule. You'll basically go week by week to see what's going to happen: 1) All-Star games, 2) Senior Bowl, 3) Shrine game, 4) the Combine, 5) the Draft. While you're on the call, they're going to write all of these dates in their planner.

Then I ask them what their school schedule looks like. Their workout schedule. They're going to tell me exactly what they're doing on each day of the week. I'm then going to tell them, "I want to talk to you every week. What day of the week will be best for you to talk to me?" Whatever day they tell me, I jot down in my calendar that my client wants to have a short five-minute conversation with me. I put that day and the time we agree on my calendar. Say it's Wednesdays. I'm going to talk to Steve every Wednesday and we're going to talk about what's going on with his training, what's going on with school, what's going on with any relationships he has, whatever it is.

This planning helps me know from the beginning, when my client is graduating from college, when they are having some big finals, when they are having a blitz day. Our weekly call accomplishes a lot and gives me a good sense of how serious my client is about their studies and their athletic goals. I get a lot of questions like, "Hey, can I go somewhere for spring break?" I might say, "No, a coach might be coming to work you out at your school, you're not going somewhere for spring break. That's not smart, you need to be training. When's your pro day?" Tell them to mark the pro day in their calendar and also mark it in your calendar and find out if the agent can attend the pro day. You're going to get all these dates in the calendar for the year and that's why this recorded strategic planning session is so important.

During the call you're going to show them when OTA's are, when mini-camp is held, when free agency begins. All those dates impact certain decisions up to the draft; here's when training camp begins, here's when all the players get cut, this is when the 53-man roster is decided, here's the 17 regular season games, here's the playoffs. So you're going to map out the whole year with the calendar. As I stated before, in the midst of all this planning, you're going to really get to know the player.

Once we're finished inserting all the calendar dates, we're going to go back to the first or second module which was about creating a brand, a core purpose, and a core message. I help them create a brand and teach them to communicate who they are and why they do what they do to the rest of the world. Through this one call I've identified what their goals are and what their schedule is going to be like for the next six to 12 months. Since I will send them a copy of the recording they can't come back to me and say, "Hey, I didn't know." Excuses do not roll in my world.

Step 9: Prepping Players/Pre-Draft Training

One of the hottest topics and biggest questions a client wants you to solve for them immediately is training. Training for the Combine, training for their pro day. This is how you need to work through this process, and how to talk to your player.

Number one, talk to them about where they want to train. When they tell you, "I want to go to Florida because there's this great trainer down there" that's when you say, "Wow, how are you going to pay for that?" This area of training is where you need to educate your players and their families. The most critical people in getting a player to the NFL are their coach and staff at their current university. A player should stay at their school and train with their own strength coach. "Why?" This is what I tell players:

"Number one, it's free. Number two, your strength coach already knows you; they know your strengths and weaknesses so they will tell you what improvements you need to make and how you need to make them. In addition to the strength coach you'll have a position coach there who can work with you so you can get better at football —after all, isn't that your goal? Also, college facilities have access to NFL film and I think it's important in preparation for your pro day and everything else that you watch current film on players in the NFL at your position and see if you have skills that would allow you to say, 'Hey can I beat that guy out?' Because that's what you have to do… beat somebody out. You go to some random gym and they aren't going to have any of that.

"That strength coach at the University is going to be a lot more qualified than any person who's got some kind of speed training or something at a gym. In fact, you don't even know what you're going to get at a gym. A lot of gym trainers are not that qualified in the performance training field. I've seen a lot of athletes go to outside training and they do not do better. They actually do worse. They should've just stayed at their school.

"It's important that you stay at your school because you need to keep your 'paycheck.' A client will respond, 'What are you talking about, I don't get a paycheck!' to which I respond, 'You need to keep your scholarship!' Stay on scholarship, get your master's, get your degree. Keep that paycheck! I don't know why any person in their right mind would leave their school, drop out of school, and not keep their scholarship check. That is leaving money on the table. That is the number biggest mistake a player makes.

"What else do you usually have at a university? A nutritionist. Go talk to your nutritionist. They might tell you that you need to gain weight or lose weight to get rid of some body fat. The nutritionist at your school will help you do that. Again, that's free.

"Or, you might say one day, 'Wow, I'm a little bit tight today, what am I going to do?' Well, at your university you've got a really nice training room, ice baths, a trainer, doctors, and maybe even a massage therapist to work the kinks out. Again, all free."

Bottom line: any agent who is telling players to train somewhere else is promoting the worst idea. It doesn't pencil. Don't do it. Don't recommend it. And if that's what the player insists on doing, then all you can do is educate them and they can pay for it or negotiate with a trainer to pay later once they get a signing bonus.

One final thought on training: If your client attends a small university and there are not a lot of fancy resources available, or the professionals they need, they can choose to go to an outside trainer but just know that you are not going to pay for it. I still find that small schools have better facilities than a gym.

Step 10: Road to the Draft/Marketing Your Clients

A lot of agents lack the desire or skill to market their clients to all the teams yet it's such an important aspect of caring for your clients and what happens to them. Why is this important? As I showed you before, there are 327 guys who are going to get invited to the Combine. That's a lot of guys. The scouts have been out, running around, probably have their list down to about 1,000 guys from thousands and thousands of guys they've evaluated.

How do I make sure that everybody has evaluated my player and likes my player? This is where the work we did earlier in helping our client create their brand and core message comes in handy because we're going to turn those pieces into a player profile. The profile will have pictures of the player and actual testimonials from their coaches that I can share with teams.

I have my own podcast so I interview my client on the podcast. Why? Because there's a lot of information that the teams don't know about my client and that they may never find out if a scout doesn't get a chance to interview or meet that particular client. Not everybody in the organization is going to meet every single player.

They don't have time. That's why an interview on my podcast is another way to bring exposure to my client.

The next thing I'm going to do is ask my client to create a highlight film for my YouTube channel. The first five clips need to be killer. That means the player needs to showcase his best plays. I've heard scouts say, "If I don't see something the first five clips, I'm done." That's why the first five clips need to really represent the great plays and great ability by the player.

Once the player has completed these tasks, and, believe me, it takes time to work through all these steps with your client, I am going to create a Constant Contact newsletter that I will probably send out at the beginning, announcing "Meet Jill's Draft Class." I'll include some information on each player. You don't necessarily have to use Constant Contact. There's Mailchimp, Active Campaign, GetResponse, and other CRM's out there that you can use that are free or relatively inexpensive. The reason I like Constant Contact is it tracks who's opening what, who clicked on what, and who's interested in certain players. I can see who didn't open the email and certain CRM emails go straight to spam, so if that happens, it means I'm going to have to email the team from my personal email.

I send out a lot of emails from January until the draft; probably two in January, two in February, and one March (results of pro day and combine, and one email in April. Here's a recap:

1: January, meet my clients.

2: Invite everyone to the Combine: NFL staff, coaches, media, current clients, and prospective clients. I'll say, "Hey, I'll be at the Combine, would love to get together with you." I always have a dinner at the Combine.

3: "I'm going to be at so-and-so's pro day, I'd love to talk to you afterward." I'm going to send another email with video from the pro day and then give them their results from the pro day. Most players go to the Combine and the pro day.

4: Last email on the results for the Combine and the pro day.

Then comes April. The next part of the marketing agenda is phone calls. I'm calling the position coach for that particular player at that particular NFL team. This takes a lot of time. I wait for them to get back to me. They tell me what they think of him and I find out where the player stands with that team. I just keep calling until they call me back, and eventually they do, or I'll call the GM, or the head of scouting. I'll call whoever I know the best AND the position coach. Sometimes it takes calling two or three people until I get to the bottom of where they see my particular player.

I send out a lot of emails, probably about eight on each player. By the time I get to the draft I make a lot of calls. I connect with them at the Senior Bowl, I connect with the teams at the Combine, and then I will connect with scouts at the pro day. And then all of a sudden it is the draft.

I usually go to the AFCA Coaches Convention to meet college coaches. I have a booth there and I find out about next year's players. If your heart isn't into putting in all that work, this is probably not the profession for you. If you wake up energized and excited to get these things done, then welcome to my world.

Step 11: Road to the Draft/Pre-Draft Analysis

I spend a lot of time analyzing the teams. It's what I would call my pre-draft analysis, and by doing this, I'm assessing the team needs. You can Google teams and find out what they need but you also have to watch free agency. I'll go through all the transactions and find out which players the teams are signing or not re-signing. I'm going to look at the team needs, the position, and the current players' salaries. How do I do that? Since I'm a member of the NFLPA, I can pull up previous salaries and I can find out what everybody's making, I can find out when their contract is coming up, figure out how old they are, figure out how many seasons they have, whether the player was drafted and how high, how much money they are making, how much money they have been given up front, and the player's stats. I'm going to look at all of these categories with my player and we're going to start to categorize teams. I have already asked my player to watch film of all the NFL teams at their current position so he's ready to start categorizing teams with me.

Let me give you an example: right tackle. I'll go around the league and I'll figure out that the Minnesota Vikings look like they're blowing out their whole offensive line, they didn't re-sign a lot of guys at right tackle, they struggled at that position, so they might be on my A Team as opposed to my B or C Team. Since my player has been watching film, I'll ask him what he thinks. "Can you beat the guy who started last year?" He says, "Oh yeah, I think I can." I then ask, "Could you beat the backup guy?" He says, "Yeah, I think I can." I respond with, "Well okay, then that would be an A Team." Or, I might say, "That team just re-signed their right tackle for five million dollars and they are really committed to him." We'll list that team as probably a B or C because they probably are not going to need a lot of right tackles which is going to make it a lot harder for my client to get drafted and/or make that team.

This is the process; I'm just going to go team by team by team and they're either going to be an A, meaning you want your client to go there, a B, meaning it's kind of in between, we're also going to wait and see who they draft and also see if they sign anybody in free agency, or a C, meaning this team doesn't need this particular position, and maybe doesn't even like my player and hasn't called. So now all the teams are categorized as A, B or C.

Then, I'm going to sub-categorize each list. For the A List it would be A1, A2, A3, A4, and A5. For instance, a team has called me about a player; they like my player and that team is on our A Team— they need what I have and they're calling my player. That team may rank up to an A1. The draft might change things. If they draft somebody high at that position, they may rank up on the A List, or they may become a B or a C.

That's how I do pre-draft. I do a lot of analysis and I talk to a lot of people. Again, I'm calling the teams all the time, I'm talking to whoever I can talk to in that organization just to gather the information to make the best decision for my player. My player could get drafted, my player could be an undrafted free agent. If your players undrafted you need to know which team, if they call, should be the first team he goes to, and it may not have anything to do with money, because the money is not going to be that big of a difference. Even the signing bonus money is not that big of a difference. I'll talk about negotiations later.

My ultimate goal is to get my client on the same page as me as far as what team, where he wants to go, what team needs him, what team likes him, and if we can get him drafted, or if we can sign him to an undrafted free agent contract.

Step 12: Road to the Draft/NFL Draft Weekend

Where your client wants to be for the draft and with who is important. I discuss this issue and educate the client and help them decide where they want to be for the draft. This is important because you don't know whether you're going to be a first-round pick, a seventh-round pick, or not picked at all. If the player wants to be around a bunch of random people who are putting a lot of pressure on him, and the crowd has unrealistic expectations, and believes he's going to be drafted really high, I will usually advise him not to hang around that group. I will tell him to stay low-key, and watch the draft with maybe a few family members. And then if you want to have a big celebration, plan for Sunday . Thursday day one of the draft the first round is picked.   Friday the second day the second, third and fourth round, and then the last day fifth round, sixth round, and seventh round. On Sunday, if something goes well, think about having a celebration. My first advice is for the player to stay low-key but that is something you would need to discuss with each client.

If you have a first-round pick, I would suggest they go to wherever the live draft is being held. If you do have a first-round pick, you would go there as well, and yes, you need to make sure your player is in a nice suit that they feel comfortable in, and they're ready for all the media attention. Anyone other than a first-round pick, I would advise a more low-key situation for my client.

If you have a first-round pick go with them to the Draft event that first day and then you can fly home for the rest of the picks. The first day of the draft I'm going to track each team's pick and monitor the team needs in case they change, and I might change my client's list based on who gets drafted. I do the same thing the second day.

I'm also calling and talking to teams during the draft, just to see what they're thinking. Are they possibly thinking about drafting my guy? Some clients might call me and say, "Hey, what teams have you heard from?" I tell them that I've heard from five teams. Let's say that a team has called me for a pick before another team can get my player—that might get a team to draft your client sooner because they want to get that player before the other team does. Needless to say, during the Draft, I'm in communication with the teams.

What happens is we get to Friday, and at this point you do an assessment of the team needs, and then on Saturday, which is the late-round picks, that goes much faster. At this point, I'm trying to keep track of everybody to see if the team assessments change, if in fact my player doesn't get drafted and I now have an undrafted free agent. Now, that is super tricky. This is a situation where you could have all 32 NFL teams calling five seconds after the draft. The system is a very, very complicated system and you need to be prepared for it. Everybody thinks their client is going to get drafted and every client thinks they're going to get drafted. Then all of a sudden they don't and you have 32 teams calling you at one time. That's why I'm back to assessing the A1, A2, A3 and so if a team calls I am ready to get a deal done and make sure my client has a place to go and has a contract.

My cell phone is charged and ready, and I'll have what I call a bat phone because I don't want to miss that all-important call for my client. When I'm waiting for a call from a team I really want to talk to, I'll give them my bat phone number. I may even have a third line depending on how many clients I have at the time. Obviously, I cannot take 32 calls at one time, and if I'm on the line with more than one team negotiating a deal and I have another client who's also waiting for a deal, it can get complicated really fast. You're going to need your team here because you'll need some help when you're communicating with your clients and the teams all at the same time. You're the only person who can talk to a team because you have to be certified. You can't have other people talk to the team.

That five minutes after the draft is dicey and you've got to be prepared, you've got to be ready, you've got to anticipate what is going to happen and guide your client through that lightning-fast situation. Once you gain some experience you'll learn how to do it, but the first time it can be extremely overwhelming if you get a lot of calls at one time for one client.

If your client does not get picked up at all, you can try to get him into a minicamp. On Sunday I might call a team and tell them, "Hey my player did not get an opportunity, do you have any minicamp spots?" You can get him into two minicamps if two different teams happen to have a minicamp on a different day, or a different weekend. The choices for your client come down to three: 1) the Draft, 2) undrafted free agent, and 3) try to get the client into a minicamp.

Step 13: Contract Negotiation/When & How to Negotiate

Scenario 1: Your client has been drafted and you need to negotiate the deal. So, how does that work? For each round, first, second, third, fourth, fifth, sixth and seventh, each spot has a slot. Let's hypothetically say your client gets drafted second-round, first pick and that spot is worth $2.5 million. The second-round second pick is also worth that amount. The person who negotiates before you, that's going to be a little bit higher, and the person who negotiates after you, that's going to be a little bit lower, so you've got to make sure that you get in that slot amount. So if that slot is worth $2.5 million, you want to hopefully try to get a little bit higher. Let's say you get

$2.6 million here and you get $2.4 million there; you've got to be in between the $2.4 million and the $2.6 million and that's what the slot is going to be worth.

Let's say one year the salary cap increases by 4%. That slot is going to hypothetically be worth about 4% more. What I usually do is wait for the agent behind me or the agent in front of me to negotiate their deal and then I make sure that, if those other two deals get done before I do my deal, I have a really good idea of where my spot is. So that's kind of how it works in negotiations with slot spots with the draft. It's really easy to figure out what your client is worth when they are drafted and there's a draft round and slot.

Scenario 2: Undrafted free agents. Each year there is a pool of about $75,000 or so to use for signing bonus money for the 20 guys teams will sign after the draft. It can be anywhere from zero to $20,000 but please don't be unrealistic. You should have previously spent a lot of time with your client assessing which team they have the best chance of making. Your client could get a minimum salary deal and some signing bonus money although the signing bonus is going to vary. I would rather have a client get less signing bonus money if they have a better chance to make the team than send them somewhere where they are loaded at that position and they are giving my client $5,000 instead of $2,000, but he basically has no chance of making the team. This is where your astute assessment and ranking of teams will come in handy!

Scenario 3: The next negotiation is your client now has played on a team for three years and has done really well so he is now a restricted free agent. In this case, they just have to do a one-year tender—they can either do the low, middle, or high. If that happens, you really don't have that much control over the negotiation. If a player has four years in, they become an undrafted free agent and now the whole league can bid on the guy. Most times if the athlete is a great player, he never even gets to free agency because that team will try to re-sign him. If they don't re-sign him, then you have to figure out what he is realistically worth and which other teams are interested in your player. When I've talked to GM's about this, they say that when a team doesn't re-sign a guy in free agency or beforehand, that's a red flag that there is something wrong. So you've got to know that you might not get as much as you think in the market because if the team doesn't re-sign him that's a red flag for other teams.

Following certain dates is really important because you can't start to renegotiate with teams until the actual free agency dates, which are shortly after the Combine. At that time, you can start negotiating and marketing your player to other teams but first you have to look at all the salaries, the production of your clients, and the numbers—you have to figure out what you think your client is worth based on what's going on in the market. I talk to my clients about all the variables; I educate them so they are realistic about what they are really worth in the market. I find that my clients almost always think they are worth more than they are actually worth. If you educate your client and show them all the salaries and explain everything to them, you'll do a much better job of renegotiating the deal with their team, or getting them a much better deal with another team.

The really important reason you need to talk to your client is to get a sense of where they are; maybe they want to stay where they are or maybe they want to go somewhere else. It's critical to always be honest and fair in your negotiations and that requires you to be in regular communication with the team and your client—that equation will equal a successful negotiation.

Step 14: Contract Negotiation/Knowing the CBA

Your client is now signed with a team and they're heading to their first minicamp. It's time to prepare them for what could happen. I call it "the big warning," which is the time when my job really matters, and that's protecting them under the current Collective Bargaining Agreement. The Collective Bargaining Agreement is a document between the union and NFL teams and it describes what the work rules are for the players.

The number one way a player can really get hurt is by not following the Collective Bargaining Agreement if they get injured. I always tell my clients before they step foot on the field with their uniform on, "You know what, if you get injured, the first person you call is me! Why? Because if you're injured, you are not really worth anything to the team, especially if you have a very severe injury. They may try to get you to sign an injury settlement which you don't ever want to agree to—there's no reason to." If a client gets injured they need to call me ASAP because we have to follow a very specific process that goes something like this: 1) You have to notify the team that you want a second medical opinion. 2) You get a second medical opinion. 3) The doctor that you go to for the second medical opinion has to provide the medical records to the team. 4) The player waits to get better. 5) When the player gets better he goes back on the field.

The player doesn't know how long it's going to be until his injury is healed and he has to see how he's doing once he's back out on the field. That's why I don't like signing injury settlements, because an injured player really doesn't know how injured he is or how long it's going to take him to get back on that field and that's what I'm talking about when I say my number one job is to protect my players under the CBA, because injuries are serious and career ending.

114

The number two way a player can get hurt is fines. You can get a fine for just about anything. Example: if your socks aren't pulled up during a game, you can get a uniform fine. If you don't tuck in your jersey properly, you can get a fine. If you try to promote a brand different than a company that has paid to be an official NFL brand, you can get fined. For example, if you try to wear an Under Armour jersey but Nike is the official sponsor of the NFL, you have to wear the Nike jersey. The player must abide by the rules or they will get fined, and if they do get fined, again, they must call their agent immediately. Why? Because as the agent you are going to need to defend them, and I have found that an agent can usually get the fine reduced. So let's say your player gets fined $15,000 for a uniform fine. The agent has to appeal that fine within a couple of days and a hearing gets set with the NFL office. I'll be on the phone with the NFL hearing officer and my player; I will defend the player and try to get their fine reduced. Since this hearing is an administrative hearing, it's just another reason why you should really be an attorney and at least understand what it's like to litigate.

In summary, the two biggest issues with my players are injury settlements (make sure your players get the injury protection benefit if they can't ever play again) and fines. Of course, there are a lot of other issues that come up that are situational, and every time an issue arises, I'll read the CBA, interpret what I think the main issue is, and I will also call the union attorneys and get their opinion, I'll talk to my client, and then decide on a course of action.

Step 15: Contract Negotiation/In-Season Work & Monitoring Injuries

Your client is playing and it's football season. I usually attend one of my client's games during the year and I also attend a lot of college games every weekend. That means during football season I'm either at a college game or an NFL game and, of course, I watch many NFL games during the season. I'll talk to my client on Monday or Tuesday and ask questions like, "How did you do? How do you think you did?" and "What do you think you can do better?"

If you have a player who didn't make a team you constantly have to be on the lookout to see who gets injured in your player's position and then call the team and also communicate with your client. Clients get really nervous when they get cut, and they get really nervous when they're not getting called. As their agent, you need to prepare them for those scenarios once the season starts. Teams tend to sign veteran guys. If a player has gone through training camp and gets cut, the team probably won't call; they more than likely get a guy who's had nfl regular season experience to come in and take over for a player whose been injured. This is why it's so important to watch all the NFL games, seeing who's injured and constantly communicating with the teams and my clients, particularly if the client is on the couch, that's a really hard place to be.

For your clients who are in play, my main focus is to encourage them, communicate with them, go to their games, watch their games, and keep in touch with their families, if they're married, and answer any questions.

Clients' Personal Development

Something I sometimes do, although not always, is to host an event where I'll bring all my clients together and I'll have a speaker come in and give a talk. One speaker might give them media training, another might teach them about branding themselves. I might have one of my former clients, now a financial advisor, come and talk to them about finances, and I might have another former client who now owns a business talk about starting their own business. I have an educational segment but I mix some fun into the event. We might go somewhere like Vegas to play golf, or another fun vacation destination.

All of the things I've talked about in this section are ways I stay close to my clients and keep connected. I think it's important to enjoy the camaraderie of my whole team of clients away from our work environments whether it's an office or a field.

Road to the Draft/Success on Social Media

It's imperative that you discuss social media with your client. They need to fully understand that what they put on their social media needs to be:

1) Appropriate. Scouts are looking at it, brands are looking at it. We've talked about building a brand and I encourage them to build their brand on Instagram, Twitter, Facebook, and LinkedIn. Follow players who are doing a great job with their social media. It's important as an agent to help clients leverage their brand so when they're done playing, they continue to utilize their name and likeness to make money for their family.

If I find one of my clients doesn't like social media, they can hire somebody to assist them with their social media networks. For instance, I have somebody who works with me by the name of Grace Dewitt, and she does take on clients separately and will help them build their social media. However they get it done, your clients need to utilize and maximize their social media because it's evolving all the time. What you can tell your client: "Don't put anything on social media that you are not okay with your grandmother seeing."

Financial Planning

So now you've got your client, you've signed your client, and your client is playing. What do you do next? I've already started the financial planning process from the beginning when I set up a ten-year plan, a five-year plan, and a one-year plan, but now that they're playing, I talk to them more about their long-term plan. One of the great things about the NFL is they have tons of bootcamps for the players, and I really encourage my players to attend these bootcamps between January and March because it's there they can network with people, they connect with people, and in fact one of the bootcamps focuses on media if they want to work for the NFL network, or if they want to be on the air. There are some bootcamps on entrepreneurialism and being in business. Once the player determines what their end game is, they can strategically choose the bootcamps that will best benefit them.

I ask my clients from the beginning, "What is your backup plan if football doesn't work out, or your career is cut short, or you retire? What other job do you want to have?" While they're playing, I try to connect them to people who are in the specific industry they've chosen. For instance, I have a client who wanted to get into commercial real estate. I introduced him to somebody who was president of a commercial real estate firm. When my client was done playing, he went to work for them, and now he has his own commercial real estate firm—this happened because of our long-term planning.

During our financial planning sessions players start to think about how they want their money to best work for them. There are a lot of financial planners out there but they need to be registered with the NFL Players Association. You, the agent, need to look at that list and make sure nobody has had any kind of trouble. The NFLPA does a background check on each of the financial planners who apply. Find out whether or not the players have had a good experience with that particular person, and then your player can start doing some small investing. The most important and immediate thing a player should do is take advantage of maxing out the amount they are putting into their 401k with the NFL, because the match is 2-1.

As an agent, you should discuss strategies to help reduce your players' tax liabilities, and then they can start to put money away. If you remember nothing else, remember this: do not ever, ever, EVER get mixed up with their money, ever, but I will say it's okay to guide them and put tools in their toolbox to equip and train them to understand and handle their own money. There are apps like Stash or Ameritrade, and Wells Fargo also has a trading account. Equip your players with tools on how to do small trades and learn how to work with money and understand money, and then assist them to secure a financial planner to advise about money. The NFLPA has a free service called Financial Finesse that is a great tool for the players. I encourage them to use that free tool. In addition the NFLPA has great guides on how to save your money.

I tell my players not to put all their financial eggs in one basket because if somebody ends up being bad, the outcome is never good. I've seen players end up with nothing at the end because they trusted the wrong people. It's my job as an agent to educate my players about money but they need to educate themselves so they can stand on their own two feet and be wise about their finances. They need to start reading, they need to save their money, not spend their money. They should definitely understand that they're going to need the money they're making now for the rest of their life. Maybe they're making a nice chunk of change right now, but it has to last them for 30 years, so it's really not that much money over the long term.

Segment III

The X's and O's of Evolution in the Sports World

Chapter 7

The Evolution of Self Within the Sports World

During my entire career, my children were around me. We had our first child, Kelly, in 1996 in New Orleans and then McKenzie in 1997 shortly after we moved to Fresno. Life is definitely a balancing act between being a coach's wife and taking care of toddlers. Being a coach's wife basically means you're doing most of the household and outside stuff on your own because your husband doesn't have an 8-5 job. I will give my husband credit for the fact that the whole time the kids were little we were at Fresno State and we intentionally stayed there for many years because we really didn't want them to change schools. He worked for Pat Hill, and we both had a great experience when john was working at Fresno State.

Things got a little bit crazy because we did move out to the property and had a lot of animals. I learned to delegate chores and tasks that I just didn't want to do. I actually hired office help which was tremendous. Living on acreage could get complicated because there were things that needed fixing out on the ranch, and we had to make sure the animals were fed, which Kelly and McKenzie usually did. Sometimes in the organized chaos of it all we would have little hiccups like the time a goat was born and had to be bottle-fed. I think the goat was in our bedroom and John was having to feed the goat at night because I was out town.

This same week we had an opposing team coach come visit with us and he just looked at John and said, "Well, I never really thought I would come visit you the night before a game and that we would be making sure to bottle feed your goat." It might have been around Thanksgiving because I remember taking the girls to my parents' for Thanksgiving and John was home. A lot of the animals were his idea anyway so it was only right that he got stuck bottle feeding a goat.

It seemed like every time I came back from out of town a new animal had made our house its home and my response was always the same: "Yikes! I don't think I can take another animal." But John liked collecting them. One time I came home after some event, probably the Combine or the Senior Bowl, or something like that, and a new horse had appeared. My husband basically told me, "Oh, that's Mr. Clovis Feed's (my husband's nickname for the feed store owner – John has special names for everyone) horse, we're just watching it for a while. "Mr. Clovis Feed" owned the feed store in town and we, of course, were very good friends with his whole family because we had so many animals.

One day I ran into Mr. Clovis Feed and said, "Hey, I think your horse has something wrong with his hoof."

He looked at me and said, "That's not my horse. That's your horse."

I was like, "What?"

"Oh yes, they bought that horse from me."

John and the girls never really liked to tell me when they bought new animals because it used to really make me really mad. My first thought was always, yikes, one more thing to take care of. But you know, we just made it work.

I didn't want to have a nanny, so John and I just figured it all out between the two of us. I had moved everything to our property and had a place right on the property where people could come to work, and that made everything a lot easier. What I love now is the internet has made everything so much easier for someone in my industry. Now that the kids are grown and gone, I have three different places where I work.

I have an office in my house that has a sound studio upstairs so I can record my podcasting episodes and shoot any kind of video for content.

I have a WeWork base in West Hollywood called The Wing, which I can use if I need a conference room, which is really cool because it's a WeWork space for women and it hosts tons of great events at night. There's a lot of professional women from the entertainment industry who use the facility. It's a great place to network with people in other industries which I really like to do, I like to learn from people in other industries. I find it more helpful to me than focusing on what my industry peers are doing, because most of the time I don't agree with how they're running their businesses. Or, I should say that most often I don't see things the way they do. I want to do it the way I want to do it.

I have another office in Shaver Lake. where we have a cabin. I turned one room into an office to where I can work during my longer stays at the cabin.

What I love so much about my job is it doesn't really matter where I am—I can get my job done anywhere. And since I like to travel so much, I really love traveling to the players' games—I'm at a football game every Saturday so I usually see players live that I'm recruiting.

When I think about my life, I realize just how lucky I've been. I have designed a life where I never feel like I'm working. I never have to be in one place all the time; I can be anywhere, and I designed my life like that on purpose. I like being self-employed. I like having the freedom to decide what I'm going to do each day and what I'm going to focus on. I don't have somebody dictating what I have to do. Now obviously, when a client has a situation, I have to deal with it; that's my job. But I think what's so great about being self-employed, and anybody who is self-employed knows this, is that you have control over your day.

Now, the other great thing about self-employment as a sports agent is you never know what's going to happen, which causes your daily life to be somewhat unpredictable. When I get a call from someone who has a problem or issue, I deal with it on my terms.

In my 30 years as a sports agent, I'm in a very different place now than I was when I was younger. In the early days, I had two children who were in school and involved in every sport and I had to coordinate all their practices and games along with being a coach's wife and going to my husband's games. For a while it was just insane and I have no idea how many miles I clocked on my car during that time. Now, we're empty nesters. Our daughters are done with college; one is married and involved in real estate and the other one just graduated from USC and is involved in Teach for America. I no longer worry about getting them to a practice or a game or being there to watch them play their sport. I don't have to worry about trying to get a babysitter when I fly out of town.

I remember when McKenzie was born and I had to go to the NFLPA meeting in Los Angeles. She was just a baby—I was still nursing and I kept thinking, how am I going to go to this event for two days and not be able to feed my baby? I also had to worry about breast milk soaking through my shirt at the event…now that was a ton of fun.

Today, I am still a coach's wife and I'll describe to you what that's like for me. The first weekend of this 2019 season USC was playing Fresno State. No fewer than 17 people called us for tickets. And, of course, John and I do whatever we can to help get tickets, which isn't always easy. When that happens, my husband and I both have what I call ticket train wrecks. This is when my husband tells five people that he can get tickets for them, and I tell five people that I can get tickets for them—but we only have six tickets. Voila! Train wreck. Since I travel a lot for work, which I love, I'll return home for the first game and John will say, "Oh, by the way, I told a friend from New York he could stay at the house, and oh yeah, I told two former players they could stay at the house, and oh yeah, I told two, no, four, of my best friends that they could stay at the house." Our daughter invited four of her friends from college to stay at the house, and all of a sudden there was quite a crowd—and they're all staying at our house. So that means now I have to figure out how I'm going to feed all these people for two days and make sure I have enough tickets.

So, for the first game of the season, our house was full of people, everybody got along well, and we all had all kinds of fun. In today's world, there are so many different dietary restrictions and allergies so I wanted to make everything compliant with what people could and couldn't eat. I made everything the day before including a big pot of chili that all we had to do was heat up. The next day we got up and even more people were coming in and out so we fed them again.

That first game was a night game—I think we finally got home at 1:30 in the morning, and everybody wanted to eat again. Out came the chili again; we heated it up and we all dug in while we watched Sports Center.

The morning after the game I had to get up, get dressed, and go out of town to a wedding and there was something like eight people —they were all over the place. I walked into my kitchen and it looked like a frat house; there was stuff everywhere. I thought okay, peace out, I'm going to the airport. My husband was asleep, everybody was asleep. Thank goodness I have really nice friends because they did the dishes and cleaned up the whole mess. John washed all the towels… and I've told you his very specific method for washing so you know it was done right…according to John.

But that's the thing, weekends during the season, at least for our family, are extremely busy. And I haven't mentioned what the mood is like if we don't win—all I can say is it's just not fun. As our daughter quips, "It's only fun when you win."

So as a coach's wife, I have to keep track of tickets, I have to get people to the game, I have to make sure that people have food, and of course you have to have everything ready for your house guests. At the Baxter house that's what home games are like. Fortunately, I'm used to it because that's how it was at our house, growing up—my parents were exactly the same way and my mom did the same stuff I see myself doing now.

Chapter 8

The Evolution of Women in the Sports World

I've been asked many times through the years if it is difficult to be a female in this business. If I can be completely transparent with you, I first started out in this business because one of my dad's players needed help so I just started helping him; I didn't realize at the time that I was the only female agent. That was 1987. I should say at least in football there weren't any other female agents and I didn't really think about it much because if you have a good client, the teams are going to want to communicate with you. They don't care if you're a male or a female. As long as you're honest and fair and you always get back to them, you're not going to have a problem.

On the team side, I have not experienced any problems dealing with any of the guys who work within the NFL teams, whether they're scouts or coaches or GM's. They've always been great to me and have treated me well. But, I am a coach's daughter and a coach's wife so I already knew a lot of the people in the industry. My relationships are different.

I think it may be a little more difficult when, as a female, you're recruiting players, and you have to get past a little of the "You're a girl" type of mentality. But once they get to know you and like you, and you connect and have the same values, I don't think players are going to care whether you're male or female. I think it comes down to values and connections. If a player wants you to get them concert tickets or go out partying with them all the time and that's not who you are, then they're not going to pick you anyways, whether you're male or female. You can discuss the female factor with a potential client if you want, but in the end, I've always felt like it's been an advantage. Why? If I'm at an event, people in the industry definitely know who I am, because for a long time there weren't very many women.

There are a lot more women agents now, and there are women in the front office, and women coaches. So we're making a lot of headway as women, but I wouldn't make it a big deal. You can address it if you sense it might be an issue. It's not like they tell you, "I'm not hiring you because you're a woman." The fact is that there are probably some men out there who won't pick you because you're a woman, or it could be that they just don't pick you because they like what someone else has to offer. Just be who you are and do the best job you can for your players and things have a way of working out just fine.

One of the most frequent questions I get asked about women in the sports industry is, "What is it like working around all those men?" I think the best way to answer that is to share three different stories about being a female versus being a male in this industry. I honestly don't think many of the people in the NFL care that much either way. I've only been treated with the utmost respect. People have been super kind to me and they respond to me if I have what they need. It's that simple.

First, in 2019, a sports reporter called me and asked, "Hey Jill do you know that the number of female agents has gone down?" I don't know what she based her research on but I asked her if she was sure and she said she was. It could be that the type of research she did revealed there were fewer female agents with an active client, or a client on the practice squad. It's hard to say because I don't know what criteria she used. What I do know is if I start out with five players with five contracts but only one of them makes it, I've only got one guy on the active roster even though I negotiated all five deals. With that in mind, there would be a perception that there's more women, but apparently right now there's not more women with active clients. There might be more women who are certified NFLPA contract advisors, but fewer women with actual clients who made a team. I do think there is a global push on the team side where they are welcoming more women in. There are more women owners in the NFL right now. So, yes, I think there are more women in football as a whole, on the team side. On the agent side not sure.

I see a big difference between me and other women in the industry. I've always worked independently. I've never worked for another agency. You might ask why. I'm married to a football coach and if you think I'm going to get involved with my peers and risk my husband's job in case one of those people makes a mistake, like they violate an NCAA rule—no thank you. I'm not doing that. Has that hurt me? I don't know. Perhaps if I had gone with a huge firm, maybe I would have acquired bigger clients earlier. I have no idea. I've always operated on my own and I like it that way—I don't do anything dishonest… ever…and I know what the rules are because I've grown up in the business. So I follow the rules, I go through the compliance officers, I meet with the players when I'm supposed to meet with them; usually after the season is complete. Honestly, I don't even like contacting players during the season although sometimes it's necessary if I need to go after a certain player.

Second, as far as the old boys network, which definitely exists, maybe I just feel very comfortable in that arena. If I walk into a room full of men, or women, I feel comfortable in both arenas. I'm a pretty social person, I like talking to people, I like meeting people, and I love learning from people. Does it bother them? I don't know. If it does, they certainly don't tell me. No one has ever treated me disrespectfully in this industry.

Now I will say this; there are some things about being a woman that are an advantage. When you're the only female they know when you're coming. I'm the only one over there—I don't look like everybody else. I consider that an advantage rather than a disadvantage.

Chapter 9

The Evolution of Adapting to a Changing Social Environment

In December 2017 I found myself frustrated with the sports agent business as a whole. The current model for being a sports agent is that the agent takes a percentage of the client's income, whether it's a player or a coach, because I represent both.

In the coaching industry I would negotiate a contract for a coach and then get a percentage of their salary, let's say 3%. That meant if a coach made $1 million dollars, I received 3% of their salary, and that would be for each year. So each year, I would send a bill and they would pay me $20,000 a year for let's say a three-year deal. Coaches didn't like that; mostly because there was sometimes no apparent evidence that I did anything for them in year two. I totally get that. When they would come to me with that kind of statement, I'd say, "Yeah you're right. Maybe last year I didn't do anything for you, but I did negotiate a deal for you and got this amount of money for you the year before." Would that coach have received the same amount without representation? I have no idea. What I will tell you is that if I was just billing the hours, it wouldn't bill out to $20,000. For coaches who are getting fired or coaches who are having a bad season and they get a $20,000 bill from an agent, and I'm just using that as an example, they will figure out some way not to pay you. That happened to me; I had two clients who just didn't want to pay. Of course, the only way for me to enforce it was to sue my client, which I didn't want to do. This is why I found myself frustrated with the system.

Concierge Model for Coaches

I gave serious thought about how to restructure the way I do business, especially with the coaches and athletic directors I represent. I looked at different business models, including the medical industry. I discovered that some doctors have moved to what is called a concierge doctor concept, where they service maybe a hundred patients and the doctor charges each patient a flat fee of $2,500 a year to be a patient. I really liked the concierge concept so I decided to transition my sports agent business to that model and honestly, I think it's the best thing I ever did. The concierge model applies to coaches. To use that model with players is a whole different can of worms because of the Collective Bargaining Agreement and the pre-determined SRA's (Standard Representation Agreement). I can tell you how to solve that problem too but let's talk a little more about coaches.

When I transitioned to a concierge agent business for coaches and administrators, I created a 25-page workbook that allows me to set up a ten-year, five-year and one-year plan. In the workbook I help them create a brand, I help them identify who they are and what they represent, I have them identify their big goal, where they want to work, who they want to work for, and why, and I help them describe and define their end game. The branding portion takes quite a bit of time because each client is different. I go through the workbook content in extensive detail with them and I also include recorded audio calls clients can save for their file. After the workbook content and audio calls, I come up with a plan for them. I am not executing the plan for my coach clients; I assist them in executing the plan and give them suggestions based on what they've told me.

For example, if I ask a current coach if they'd like to be an NFL coach or a college coach, and they say, "Oh, I definitely want to be in the NFL," and they're coaching in a Division II school, we have to figure out how we are going to get them connected into the NFL if they don't know anybody. Or, we might talk about how to get them in a higher division so they can get more exposure that allows them to connect with people in alignment with their end goal. Once I get my clients to focus on what they want, I can accurately guide them.

If the coach client is on a college campus there are scouts coming in every day to look at the players. That's another group they would want to connect with. For a coach client at a Division II school, you won't have a lot of scouts coming in to evaluate talent, therefore, you won't have as much access to people in the NFL. No matter what division or school, getting in the NFL is difficult because it's a bad numbers game. There are only 32 teams and the number of coaches on each team as of 2018 ranges from 28 (Buffalo Bills) to 14 (New England Patriots). The open spots are limited and the competition fierce.

Shifting my business to a concierge business has also allowed me to represent everybody, and what I mean by that is, I don't care if you're the head coach of the New England Patriots or you're the GA at McNeese State—every client is getting charged the same. And each year the coach client will repay the yearly flat fee if they want me to represent them.

And what am I doing for them throughout the year? I'm assisting them with their job searches. If there is a job opening and they want to apply, I create an industry-specific polished resume that highlights their expertise and qualifications. I create a profile for them and keep it updated. When a job comes open, my client is armed and dangerous and ready to submit all their information; they're not scrambling to update everything at the last minute. They'll have a personal brand that best represents them so they can go into an interview confident and prepared.

I also negotiate their deal for them. I do all this for the one flat fee. If a client says, "Geez, Jill, I don't want to do all that because I have another option," in that case I will tell them, "If you want me to negotiate a deal, I will do that on a sliding scale based on what the contract is worth."

Those are the two options I now offer clients; concierge and sliding scale based on contract worth. Most of my clients have picked what I call the flat fee model and it's been very successful. I have one client who was coaching at a Division II school in Wisconsin, and within two weeks of him focusing on what his goals were, he ended up at a Division I school and that's exactly what he wanted. Once he consulted with me and got clear on his goal, he called somebody he knew at the Division I school; there happened to be an opening and he got the job. Had he not talked to me I don't think he would have focused on going after that because at first he didn't know exactly what to do to get what he wanted.

With my new business model, my clients are happier, and I'm happier. Previously, what had been frustrating as an agent is I do a lot of work but if somebody doesn't get a job I don't get paid. In the new model, I get my flat fee up front and they are getting representation with clear goals for a reasonable and fair fee. In addition, how much the client will potentially make is taken out of the equation. Everyone is paying the same amount each year. I no longer worry about the ups and downs of this profession. I can focus on my clients' goals and try to connect them to the people they will need to accomplish their goals. They can't come back to me and say, "I don't think you did enough."

When those two coaches did not pay me, to be honest, I was very upset because they had signed a contract, and then breached the contract. However I learned a great lesson. Expectations: They both had unrealistic expectations as to what a sports law attorney actually can do. A sports agent doesn't have control over wins and losses and doesn't have control over who is going to hire whom. I might be able to introduce you to someone you didn't know before. I can certainly negotiate and protect you contractually. But who you know is more important than who I know. I have 30 years of experience. I deserve to be paid but I also think we all need to charge a fair fee.

Concierge Model for Players

I've discussed how the concierge model works for the coaches and athletic administrators I represent but now I want to turn your attention to how it works for players.

Players also feel like they pay too much to their agents. The bottom line is coaches and players don't like paying their agent's bill. In fact, they hate it. When it came to a new model for representing players, I begin the meeting and discuss the actual amount they will pay an agent. I explain the money side—I lead with that conversation. I ask them if they knew that the industry standard for an agent was 3%. We have a discussion about the financial aspect of paying an agent to represent them. In thinking about all of this, I asked myself how can I make my service more affordable for a player? A couple of things stood out. If a player needs a renegotiation, and I'm not talking about one of my players but one who comes to me from the outside, they can choose my sliding scale. This works if they just want a deal negotiated and don't want somebody to represent them during the year. The problem with that is if they get hurt or they get a fine they really do need an agent to coordinate everything for them, and they need to follow the CBA. The sliding scale works as long as they don't want anything beyond the negotiation. Voila the idea. Sign them to an SRA so they are protected. Each year I can apply the agreed-upon flat fee which obviously can't exceed the 3% and won't be paid unless they make the 53-man roster. This way there are no surprises. Obviously if the signing bonus is high enough and the flat fee doesn't exceed the 3% the fee will have already been paid.

For players who are entering the draft, I'm going to charge them based on their draft status. If they are an undrafted free agent who's projected to make minimum salary, they're going to pay a higher percentage—that's an industry standard, but if they start to ask for money for this and that which I consider an inducement this model will not work. If they're a first-round draft pick I can charge a lower percentage, or work out a flat fee. I find the new concierge model to be flexible and fair based on what I think the time commitment is going to be and what the player projections are in the draft.

Staying Relevant in Today's Social Environment

It's so important to stay in step with the times. That means that those who are averse to social media and other present-day tools are going to be at a distinct disadvantage if they want to grow their business. I mentioned Chalene Johnson's Build Your Tribe podcast earlier, but I have to say her Marketing Impact Academy is fantastic and well worth the investment of time and effort. I make it a point to study people who are not in my industry and what they're doing in marketing and their businesses. When I went to Chalene's conference the first time I had two huge a-ha moments.

First, I knew I needed to start a podcast. I liked the idea of a podcast because I can audio record in my sweats without having to worry about hair or makeup. I ordered an online course on how to do a podcast and I followed it to a tee. It's been a really good, positive influence. (Pat Flynn's Power Up Podcasting is the online course I followed.)

Second, I knew I needed to create online courses to educate and empower my clients. The reason for this is because once or twice a week, sometimes more, I get an email from a player and the message is pretty much the same: "I know I can play in the NFL; I need you to represent me, here is my YouTube video. Oh, and I've been out of college for two years but I know I'm good enough."

Well, to be honest, at this point, I am not going to take on somebody who has been out of college for two years, didn't get an opportunity in the NFL from the beginning, and now is looking for representation. That is not going to be a good use of my time. The CBA requires an athlete to pay the agent fee once they make an active roster and the odds are not good that a player who emails me with his plea is going to make it on an active roster.

With that in mind, I created an online course entitle The X's and O's of How to Represent Yourself. I tell athletes how I go through the process—all a player has to do is follow my instructions to a tee and they can market themselves to the NFL and see what kind of feedback they get, although my guess is that they're probably not going to get the reaction they're looking for. But hey, maybe they will. It happens. If a player believes in themselves and their skills and abilities, then they should take a stab at representing themselves. The harsh reality is that the NFL is looking for draft picks. That's just the way it is.

As an agent, the biggest waste of time is when I spend a lot of time trying to get a prospective client a "job" meaning an active roster position, and they don't get in. These are guys who are actually on the NFL's radar, yet they just don't make it either.

Why would a talented player not make an NFL team? Again, it comes down to the same old math problem: Each year 775 new guys sign an NFL contract and only 176 new players make the final cut. Doesn't make for very good odds so a player who wants to represent themselves must firmly grasp this reality before they spend significant time and effort. My online course is designed to guide a player through the process with a paint-by-number system.

I have created and will continue to create online courses to help me execute my job. Often, people come to me with, "Hey I want to be a sports agent." Rather than spending three hours on the phone, I created an online course, which is The X's and O's of Representing NFL Players, which you read in Segment II of this book. (www.jillmcbridebaxter.com) My online course will help you avoid making the same mistakes I made: Don't waste your time on clients who are never going to pay you. Don't waste your time on clients who are never going to execute what you're telling them.

I'll continue to add courses that are relevant to the industry. Thus far I have four online courses:

1) The X's and O's of Representing NFL Players

2) The X's and O's of How to Represent Yourself

3) How to make healthy food for a large group of guests. Remember, I don't like cooking so I need a lot of help in this area, which is why my friend Maggie is the hostess. She shows you how to make crowd-sized dishes fast, efficiently, and economically.

4) Academic Gameplan 101 for students who are struggling academically (www.academicgameplan.com).

My online courses save me a lot of time and yet allow me to share my knowledge and experience with the world. (jillmcbridebaxter.com)

Chapter 10

The Evolution of the Sports Business as a Whole

I think the primary way the business has really evolved is how the expectations of players have changed over time. These days, they are really expecting me to pay for a lot of their out-of-pocket expenses but it doesn't pencil for lower rounds and undrafted free agents. In addition I don't like setting a precedent for being treated like a bank instead of what I am, which is an attorney. The concept is they are hiring a professional and the professional gets paid. The recruiting process with my competitors unfortunately has created an atmosphere where players and families want to see what they can get from the agent. I just don't feel comfortable with what I consider to be an inducement mentality. Do I not get players because of it? I don't know, probably.

I believe the concierge concept as a whole is a much better way to do business, at least with coaches, and administrators it is. I can represent a lot more people using this model. I do know that I have enjoyed doing business so much more since I shifted to the concierge model rather than telling clients, "Okay, I'm going to sign a three-year deal and let's see if you get a job and then I'll negotiate the deal and then you owe me this much money." They didn't like that, and to be honest with you, it didn't feel good to us either. My husband and I hired somebody because he was applying for some head coaching jobs, and he ended up getting all the jobs on his own. I ended up looking over the deals and making sure they were all right.

I experienced another a-ha moment a couple years ago when my husband asked me one day, "Who are you and what do you represent?" He's really into studying brands and how they work. His question made me stop in my tracks and really think what gets me up every morning? I had to ask myself what makes me excited about what I do? I'm all about protection, advocacy and trust. Asking those questions defined who I am and what I do for my clients. It's the first thing I tell clients when I meet with them. "I am about protection, advocacy and trust." I want to make sure every day that I'm protecting you, that I'm an advocate for you, and that you have a trusted advisor. I want them to know I'm going to be there for them. I tell them, "I don't care if it's the middle of the night, you can call me, not a big deal."

***

I want to wrap up by sharing two stories about my clients. By reading these accounts you'll understand why people need a sports agent, or maybe your interest will be piqued and you'll want to become a sports agent. These are great stories, although they didn't start out so great.

The first story is about a coach who received a new job and contract at a new university. To finish his deal at the new school, we had to review his deal at the old university. When I reviewed his old deal, the contract said that if the head coach left the current school, all the assistants' contracts would only be valid for 30 days. Of course the coaches didn't notice until the coach left. The coach's present school had been successful, they had even gone to the Rose Bowl that year. All of a sudden the head coach gets a better job and leaves, yet not everybody goes with him. My coach-client did have an opportunity to go with him, but at the same time, was offered a job at another university. When he got the contract he looked at it and thought, this is really not what I agreed to. The contract was for a three-year deal but it had a six-month buy-out, which really is a six-month deal. He recognized the six-month clause and called me right away. He said, "This isn't right, this is not what I agreed to." I renegotiated with the university to make sure it was a true three-year deal and he was making a lot of money.

After year one he was a defensive coordinator. His side of the ball didn't do well and the new head coach decided to get rid of him after just one season. Because the university owed this particular coordinator so much money, the other coaches didn't get their contracts changed. So then the school tried another little tactic; let's not fire him, let's force him to quit. So they stuck him in an office, and, by the way, this is a horrible thing to do to a coach. The school acted like he was still on the staff and then hired somebody to replace him as coordinator. That's when he called me because they owed him somewhere around $1 million at this point and they didn't want to pay him. I told him, "You've just got to sit it out and wait, because in order for you to get the buy-out money, the university is going to have to terminate you." He waited. He diligently went into work every day as hard as it was for him. I mentioned to somebody on that campus, "By the way you're creating a very hostile work environment for my client." They finally terminated him, without cause by the way. He got the money owed to him. But had he not called me he would have not had his contract changed and he would have lost $1 million.

I'm talking specifically to coaches now—your contract might be fine, but just make sure you have an attorney look it over and tell you either it's fine, or that it's not fine. The scenario I just told you happens time and time again. Protection. Advocacy. Trust. Again, that's my promise to my clients and it's my mission to make sure they are protected on all fronts.

Coaches have also come to me after they've already signed a contract. I review it and deliver the news, "Yeah, this isn't too great, but at this point there's nothing you can do about it. At least you know now and you're not going to get blindsided if there's something bad in there that doesn't protect you properly."

Contracts are huge concerns for coaches and coaching families. It concerns me because universities are interested in saving money and they'll do anything to protect their bottom line. I don't care how much money the university has; they will always try to save their bottom line.

I will share another story with you. I share it to demonstrate that employees in athletics, especially, need representation. Interestingly enough, a year later, another client, working for the same school as in the story above, same CFO, is trying to get out of another client's contract. I negotiated the deal, and thank goodness, got all the buy-out money, and my client got another job right away. But again, the same school tried to get out of the payment. Same CFO. That CFO later ended up getting fired.

Everybody thinks universities have so much money but it's expensive to run a university. When they fire an entire staff, they're going to try to figure out a way to save money and that includes doing their best to not pay the buyouts.

I tell coaches all the time, "Protect yourself because it's a very insecure business. There's a lot of money at stake and you don't want your family to be left high and dry. The minute your contract ends, no matter what, your health insurance ends usually at the end of that month. So you have to be prepared for that if you have a family and you don't know when you're going to get your next job." Another reason coaches need representation.

There was another serious situation with the same client who had the bad situation at the university that forced him to report in daily to the football office after he had been fired. Not comfortable.

He goes to another school, and he's faced with yet another really bad situation. One of the players died, and all of a sudden the school is conducting an informal investigation, they're on a fact-finding mission. The coach called me to ask, "Should I go in and talk to them?" I told him, "No, don't talk to them." I added, "You can't be insubordinate to your contract, so what you do is you go in and say, 'Hello, I am a coach here, and if you have questions for me I would like for you to put them in writing and I will respond in writing to make sure I give you accurate information.'"

Thankfully, he listened to me and the school never even submitted any written questions. If he had consented, his answers would have been public knowledge, because that's how it is with any public institution.

My point is: if you're a coach, you're a coach. If you're an attorney, you're an attorney. Get advice from an attorney, not a coach.

I wouldn't go on the field and start coaching the O-line because that's not what I do.

Now I might tell my husband what to do as a Special Teams Coordinator. I'll say to him, "Now that play was not a good idea," and he'll immediately retort, "Well, did you watch the film?" I'll respond, "No, but hey, I'm just suggesting." He gets super mad at me when I do that.

The truth is that I sometimes do know how so-and-so matched up against so-and-so. No, I didn't watch the game film—I watched the game. Everybody has an opinion about the games, but unless you're in the trenches, you really don't know.

That brings up my mom. When we were growing up and a visitor would spout their opinion to my mother at a game or after a game, she'd look at them with a sweet little smile on her face and say, "We love you but you don't know what the f**k you're talking about." My mom could get away with saying something like that because there was that sweet smile on her face when she said it.

Conclusion

Thank you for reading this book. My final charge to you is this: if you want to be a sports agent, go for it! I've given you the exact tools in Segment II to make it happen. I do think it's more difficult to do it how I did it, where I went off on my own and just started. When I started 30 years ago, one of my dad's players needed help as I said at the beginning of the book, and that's how I got into it.

If you're going to be a sports agent, you first need to decide who you are and what you represent. And then you need to find clients who value the same character traits that you value. When those two elements are in alignment, you can be successful. If being a sports agent is what you want to do, do it; just don't quit your day job until you build up your business. I've been fortunate my husband brings in a steady paycheck but if you don't have that luxury, plan, save, and build up your client base before you go full-time. In the sports agent business, you eat what you kill, that's the way it goes.

If you're just entering into the coaching world, or you're a coach's wife, just know there are a lot of up and downs in that world. You've read Paulette's story so you know the dangers of what can happen.

If you're an athlete save your money. You never know when your athletic career will end. Always be planning for your next career.

If you're a fan at the games, be mindful of who is sitting around you. You might have a parent next to you whose kid is on the field. You might have a coach's kid in front of you. You might have an administrator's kid in front of you, or somebody's dad, somebody's son, somebody's sibling. Everybody on that team and coaching staff is trying to do their best; they love football and everybody wants to win. I know you're there to be a fan, I know you are paying for your ticket and you are there to be entertained but just know that it's hurtful to those who may be sitting around you when you make negative comments.

Go out there and do what you want to do in life. It's yours for the taking!

About the Author

Jill Mcbride Baxter

The daughter of University of Utah Hall of Fame football coach Ron Mcbride, Jill Mcbride Baxter was born into a sports family. She's combined her love for the game with her passion for the law to become a leading sports agent and attorney. She's been representing professional football players, coaches, media and college athletic administrators for nearly 30 years.

Jill spent her childhood on the football practice fields and in and around coaches' offices. She's married to a highly successful college coach, USC assistant John Baxter. Needless to say, her network in NFL and college football is second to none.

She's an aggressive negotiator for her clients. Her core values are: Protection, Advocacy and Trust. She aligns herself with like-minded clients, which makes it easy to fight for their best interests. Through accurate research, resources, integrity, determination, and experience, Baxter knows how to negotiate and get the best deal for her clients.

She provides support and counsel for her clients in a unique and personal manner. Her clients quickly become family.

"Jill Baxter has been one of the most critical support systems in my NFL career. She has been in my corner since Day One. Not just helping me with football-related issues but also the obstacles that life has thrown at me."

Former Cleveland Browns Receiver Marlon Moore

"While Jill is a veteran in Sports Representation, she is anything but old school. She is constantly seeking innovative way to serve her clients, it's why she brought me on board.

Grace DeWitt, Digital Marketing Strategist, founder of Douglas Digital.

She has worked with general managers, player personnel directors, head and position coaches, and scouts from all 32 NFL teams, as well as many CFL, UFL, and Arena League teams. Those contacts are essential in representation and negotiation sessions. As a practicing attorney, she is well versed in contract negotiations, the sports media industry, and employment law.

Baxter is completely familiar with the NFL's Collective Bargaining Agreement (CBA) and uses it to protect her clients in times of injury or crisis situations.

Jill is married to John Baxter, USC assistant coach, and they have two daughters, Kelly and McKenzie. She is a graduate of the University of Utah and earned her Law Degree from the University of the Pacific McGeorge School of Law. She is certified as an agent by the NFLPA and has passed the bar and can practice law in Arizona, Maryland and Utah.

Acknowledgements

Thanks to Michelle Hill, Your Legacy Builder at Winning Proof, for taking my dictated words and turning them into this book, and for the multiple phone calls and discussions. Thank you to Michelle's team of experts: Michael Scott, the cover designer who took a photo and some words and made them a work of art; our transcriber, Stacey Miner who diligently and quickly transcribed my dictated story; and last but not least, the lightning fast proofreader, Michael LaRocca. To Meredith Jenks, a coach's wife and photographer, who did a photo shoot for me last spring and one of her pictures ended up being perfect for the book cover.

Thank you Grace DeWitt, digital marketing strategist, founder of Douglas Digital, the best decision I made was to add you to my team. Grace has impacted my business in so many positive ways and has served as a wonderful sounding board during the book writing and marketing process.

My best friend Judge Kristi Kapetan who I can call at any time and ask her what she thinks about just about anything. My best friend Melinda Cerisano, United Airline Pilot, who navigated countless phone calls discussing the title or content of the book. My mom, who remembers details and accuracy of stories from my childhood and gave me feedback on all my title and subtitle ideas. Thank you mom for helping raise our kids and being there for everyone. My brother-in-law Mark Redican who I call the saint, for giving me input on all the title and subtitle ideas. Thanks Dad for helping me evaluate players, recommending clients, and our many athletic adventures. Whether it was backgammon, racquetball, windsurfing, or golf we both were going to compete until the bitter end! To my brother Mike McBride and my sister-in-law Kathy McBride: thanks for housing me when I visit ASU to meet with players! Thank you to my brother Danny for talking about baseball whenever I would start down the path of possibly representing baseball players.

My sister Kelly is such an integral part of our kids life. Our girls Kelly and Mckenzie run everything by Aunt Kelly. Thanks for being there for all of us Aunt Kelly. You are a rock of strength and wisdom to everyone.

To my husband John who gave me the space during the volatile football season to escape to the cabin to complete the book and gave me detailed input on subtitle ideas. To our daughter Kelly I am so proud that you are working for Teach for America and helping to inspire and educate our youth, while you work on your master's degree and teaching credential. To our daughter McKenzie Baxter, I love talking business ideas with you and so proud of how your real estate business has grown and your love for animals always makes life interesting.

How to Contact Jill

To secure Jill McBride Baxter to speak at your team meeting, leadership meeting, conference, or retreat, to order bulk copies, or to request media interviews:

Website: https://www.jillmcbridebaxter.com

Phone: 559-250-0151

Email: jillbaxter@me.com

Do you need an Agent?

https://www.jillmcbridebaxter.com/contact-me-form

Social Media:

Subscribe to Jill's podcast Representation Without Taxation

https://podcasts.apple.com/us/podcast/representation-without-taxation/id1356954624

Instagram @agent_mcbridebaxter

twitter @J_McBrideBaxter

Facebook @jillmcbridebaxtersportsagent

If you're a fan of this book please tell others...

- Write about Born to be a Sports Agent on your blog and social media channels.
- Suggest this book to your friends, family, neighbors, and coworkers.
- Write a positive review on Amazon.com.
- Purchase additional copies for your team, conference, or to give away as gifts.
- Feature Jill on your radio or television broadcast.

Made in the USA
San Bernardino, CA
23 December 2019